Bus Touring

A GUIDE TO CHARTER VACATIONS,

U.S.A.

Bus Touring

A GUIDE TO CHARTER VACATIONS,

U.S.A.

BY STUART WARREN

with Douglas Bloch

John Muir Publications

Santa Fe, New Mexico

John Muir Publications, P.O. Box 613, Santa Fe, NM 87504

Printed in the United States of America

First edition. Second printing

Photo credits: p.44—courtesy California Bureau of Reclamation; p.46—courtesy California Office of Tourism; p.48—courtesy Tom Myers; p.50—courtesy Dr. R. W. Brumbaugh; p.63—courtesy Jeff Myers. All other photographs courtesy Maupintour.

Cover by Jim Finnell
Design by Joanna Hill

Library of Congress Cataloging in Publication Data

Warren, Stuart, 1949-
Bus touring.

1. United States—Description and travel—
1981- —Guide-books. 2. Bus travel—United States—
Guide-books. I. Bloch, Douglas, 1949- .II. Title.
E158.W37 1988 917.3'04927 88-61653
ISBN 0-912528-95-8

Distributed to the book trade by:
W. W. Norton & Company, Inc.
New York, New York

This book is dedicated to all the tour travelers who shared their journeys with me and kept me coming back for more.

Contents

Preface and Acknowledgments

Back in college, I hitchhiked home for the holidays. I'd meet locals who'd tell me why that canyon was colored red or how the little town we'd pass had come to have a name like Drain or Noti. In time, I found myself sharing these same tidbits with my friends and family. The thought of communicating my knowledge professionally came to me as a senior in college while visiting a national park where bus tours were a common sight.

Now, a decade later, I can look back on many miles of helping people enjoy the redwoods, the Liberty Bell, and other shrines of pilgrimage on the American landscape. It is always a revelation to witness the childlike curiosity in the faces of folks older than my own grandparents. Thanks to the tourists' own wealth of experiences, I often went home having learned more information than I had imparted.

This book will befriend you as an explorer by bus. I offer it in hope that this growing tradition of motor coach tourism continues to flourish.

The origin of *Bus Touring* began in the home of Douglas Bloch, who oversaw its conception, subsequent editing, and production. Prior to this time, many thousands of miles working as a director for Tauck Tours provided me with substantial research material for *Bus Touring*. The Tauck family and organization continued to play a vital role in offering me their comments, resources, and support. Larry Deckman's creative insight was invaluable to the "Tour Talk" section. Dan Conner's crystalline prose and firsthand experience living in Dixie made "Southern Comforts" a reality. The general comments of Jennifer Gehr, Ted Long and Mike Possman brought the perspective of fellow road-warriors to the manuscript.

Kudos also go to Dale Vestal and Paul Kerstetter of Maupintour, whose assistance in procuring tour-destination photos proved invaluable. Thanks also to Pete Anderson and Joe Kearney of the National Tour Association for their advice and vital assistance in this effort. The encouragement and backing of the National Tour Association helped get this work off the ground. The Computer Ladies, Casey and Berdell, were also there throughout the writing process, assisting in both production and morale.

An extra special thanks goes to my parents who imbued in me an appreciation of travel and a love of words.

Lastly I'd like to thank Steven Cary, Toni Drew, Victoria Rogers, and the rest of the folks at John Muir Publications for their terrific efforts, unfailing patience, and good humor in bringing this book to fruition.

Stuart Warren

I would like to thank the people at Graphic Arts Publishing, Ross Eberman and Doug Pfeiffer, for their initial encouragement when *Bus Touring* was still in its incipient stages.

Lori Nelson of the California Office of Tourism was most cooperative in providing photographs of northern California, the redwoods, and the wine country.

Thanks as always go to my wife, Joan, and to my parents for their continued support of my writing and publishing efforts.

Douglas Bloch

Introduction

A quiet revolution is occurring in the travel industry. Slowly but surely, domestic motor coach tour bookings have spawned a $10.5-billion business.

It wasn't always this way. Arthur Tauck ran the first New England charter in 1925 with a seven-seater Studebaker touring car. To make ends meet during the depression, Mr. Tauck sold coin trays to banks along the tour route. It didn't take long, however, for the tour industry's concept of going-in-style at an affordable price to catch on. In the decades that followed, improved creature comforts along the road and the impetus of postwar prosperity planted the seeds for the boom years ahead.

Today this mode of conveyance is no longer the recourse of the unsophisticated voyager interested in a no-frills vacation. Instead, a seat on a motor coach tour is comparable to a parlor car from the era of first-class train travel. Wraparound polarized windows, footrests, stereophonic music, overhead compartments for hand luggage, reclining seats, and a wet bar are some of the amenities that have made these vehicles the Orient Express of two-lane blacktop.

Nowadays, numerous options are available to suit the varied

tastes of a more worldly traveling public. Everything from helicopter excursions in the Canadian Rockies to narrow gauge railroad trips through the first mining towns of the Old West are successfully integrated into conventional overland tours. In the same vein, specific tours built around a single theme—such as adventure, history, and foliage—now provide an option for travelers with special interests.

Best of all, touring by motor coach represents the most value for your travel dollar. Tour operators pass on volume discounts to their clientele, enabling them to enjoy first-class meals and lodging arrangements at a fraction of what it costs nontour travelers. Moreover, charter bookings are often privy to accommodations in key destinations that the independent traveler couldn't hope to procure. Add such intangibles as the camaraderie of traveling with a group to the expert services of a driver/guide who has been there before and you have the perfect ingredients for a *bon voyage.*

Bus Touring: A Guide to Charter Vacations, U.S.A. is written to help you savor this banquet. To begin, a notion of the styles and procedures of the major tour operators is presented, followed by advice on how to interact with your travel agent and select a tour. Tips on packing, health, and other practical concerns round out the discussion on pretrip preparation. This procedural information is complemented by seasonal data on crowd and weather patterns, flora and fauna, routing logistics, cuisine, shopping, and a region-by-region description of ambience and points of interest.

From autumn in New England to springtime in the Rockies, knowing what's happening where and when enables you to determine the best time to schedule your tour and get rolling.

I

Pretrip Preparations

CHAPTER 1

Before You Board

The mortgage is paid off. With the kids gone, you enjoy a nice income. There is more than enough of everything, including time.

Travel has always had an appeal, but it all seems so complicated. Who wants to fight traffic and drive on unfamiliar roads? And with the price of food and lodging so high, it just seems more trouble than it's worth.

Sound familiar? Not if you've experienced the carefree mode of travel that allows you to get out of the armchair and onto the road. Touring America by motor coach is the most reliable, and could well be the safest, way to enjoy the many appeals of travel. At any rate, it's fast becoming the medium of choice for millions of mature travelers, as well as a growing number of younger people. With the time and energy demanded to plan and execute independent journeys, the busy working person or active retiree increasingly looks to tours as a way to travel.

It's not hard to figure out why. On a tour you'll meet new people and share travel discoveries for as long as several weeks at a time. On a guided tour you'll effortlessly learn about an exotic locale. Whether it's the revelation of looking up at a redwood or making the acquaintance of people from other parts of the world, a motor coach tour yields enrichment and renewal that lasts long after the trip is over.

Hooking up with a tour company is as easy as contacting a reputable travel agent. Their knowledge and literature help to get your tour planning process started. After determining when and where you want to go and in what style you want to travel, the agent can make suggestions and provide you with brochures.

Sound easy? While this kind of spadework requires little effort, the choices that commonly arise in the actual decision-making can often seem overwhelming. Whether attempting to navigate tricky currents in the ocean of brochure jargon or trying to determine the optimum month to avoid the crowds, most folks tend to come away with more questions than answers.

Before I address the multitude of concerns and misconceptions surrounding motor coach tours, let's look at the subject in light of the best and worst expectations.

First the good news. A bus tour at its best is a traveler's movable feast whose sweet aftertaste will linger long after the trip is over. While being transported in a chartered rolling home to some of the most compelling places on the planet sounds idyllic, the tour experience can be even more. The lifelong friendships that often begin in this milieu can emerge as the most treasured mementos of the trip. In short, tour travel can be an antidote to a humdrum and stressful existence. And even if you're already living the good life, a break in routine will broaden your outlook on the world.

The bad news is that a tour is not always a vacation. Those mornings requiring a sunrise call after an ambitious day of sightseeing may have you bemoaning the fast pace of tour travel. At such times, try to remember the famous wilderness explorer John Muir, who spoke of the necessity of expending effort to appreciate beauty. In other words, you can sleep when you get home. Furthermore, if you are expecting the rhythms of the trip and your accommodations to be just like home, you'll need to

An early morning departure is sometimes difficult after an ambitious day of sightseeing—but leave the driving to us!

make a few adjustments. This kind of travel places a premium on flexibility—the kind that lets a tough steak served by an even tougher waitress at the Grand Canyon be forgotten amidst the rapture of one of the wonders of the world. Being adaptable also extends to the sphere of social relations. Misanthropes beware! There are few places to hide! Nonetheless, enough flexibility exists in current tour arrangements to accommodate a wide range of personality types, including the introvert and late sleeper.

Whatever your personal expectations, there are certain criteria relating to itinerary, dollar value, standards of comfort, and life aboard the coach that must be understood in order to evaluate a tour package. To this end, the rest of this chapter will familiarize you with the standard operating procedures of a well-run tour.

Life Aboard the Coach

For those of you who've never been on a tour, it's important to realize that no tour purports to show you everything. Rather, the goal of most motor-coach packages is to give a taste of a region . . . hopefully a gourmet taste. Just as brevity is the soul of wisdom, ofttimes tour planners focus on the comprehensive view. The demands of time and a broad-based clientele with different interests dictate this outlook.

The Motor Coach Environment

What can you expect in your rolling home for the first week or two of touring? Don't leave this aspect of daily comfort to chance, as a good deal of time is spent aboard the coach. To assess life aboard the coach, begin by finding out something about the vehicle you'll be traveling on—whether or not seat rotation is used, if smoking is permitted, how many passengers are aboard, and so on. Let's begin with one of the most important factors—seating on the coach.

Seating Arrangements

Here's what you can expect from the most reputable companies. First, most employ a seat rotation, which allows exceptions only with a small group. On a full day of travel aboard a typical forty-seven-seat motor coach, places are generally rotated twice daily. This allows you to vary your views and meet new faces across the aisle. Charters often sell out with forty-two or forty-four passengers aboard. The empty seats that remain include the front seat, reserved for the tour director, and the back three seats, where the view to the right is blocked by the restroom.

Is there in fact a difference between seats on the coach? In the majority of American-made vehicles, the answer is "yes." Less legroom in front and the inability to recline the back seat on the door side (the back three seats on the driver's side are seldom used) represent the major deviations from an otherwise consistent level of comfort. These days, with the introduction of foreign buses into the market, the latter might not always apply. British Leylands, Belgian Van Hools, German Setras, and Canadian Prevosts all hit the U.S. tour scene in a big way in 1987. Each has its respective advantages and disadvantages. As to whether or not they surpass their American counterparts, it's difficult to say.

For what it's worth, the word on the grapevine is that the imports are "user-friendly," offering an expanded field of vision (one generally sits higher on a foreign bus) and occasionally such amenities as televisions and a wet bar. Most foreign rigs have American-made engines and parts, so servicing and repairs usually do not present a problem. Already MCI, the leading American bus manufacturer, has introduced various luxurious refinements in its new models to keep pace with these imports. When motor coach tour travel assumes the same stature here as in Europe, the traveling public can look forward to more innovations in coach design and comfort.

Health and Comfort

Regarding the restrooms, you'll be advised to use them with discretion. The reason for this is that most itineraries go off-the-beaten-track and the coach cannot be serviced. There are enough stops (a minimum of one every two and a half hours by ICC law) to take care of personal needs. Given that smoking is often prohibited by law or company policy aboard the coach, smokers also benefit from the frequent stops. More often there is a sightseeing or comfort stop every hour.

While a good itinerary is often paced to accommodate medical conditions such as low blood sugar and prostate problems, those seriously afflicted can be guaranteed relief by forewarning their tour company. If your agent enters these restrictions into the computer at the time of booking a ticket, the medical information can then be passed on to the director.

The luxurious comfort of motor coaches today will delight people who haven't used this mode of travel for some time.

A quick mention of health-related obstacles and potentially adverse weather conditions is in order. From the personal experience of the author, the consideration most often underestimated by the mature traveler is adverse effects of altitude. Consider such popular destinations as the Grand Canyon and Yellowstone, which are more than 7,000 feet above sea level. Many seniors who attempt a level of activity comparable to their sea-level pace experience shortness of breath and a quickened pulse.

When you add the subtle stresses of travel (e.g., different food and water, long periods of sitting, irregular schedules, etc.) the effects of the thinner air are sometimes exacerbated to the point where the nausea and headaches of altitude sickness can result. Medication can help after the fact, but pacing yourself very carefully beforehand, drinking lots of water, and avoiding alcohol is best to avoid this unpleasant malady altogether.

After two days, your respiratory and cardiovascular systems can often adjust to the reduced oxygen, but by then most tours will be on the road again. In general, altitude problems seldom present themselves below 6,000 feet in elevation.

Mark Twain once said, "Everyone complains about the weather but nobody does anything about it!" Well, on a motor coach, you can. If air-conditioning bothers you, take a wrap aboard to make your own adjustments to temperature on the bus. Obviously neither can the coach be adjusted to fit everyone's personal rate of circulation nor can the hot air produced by complaints warm things up with the same efficiency as a sweater.

It might be a good idea to take along a water bottle. While most itineraries have stops with water available, at times this isn't the case. If you take medication, this can be especially unnerving as the water in motor coach restrooms is not always drinkable.

Regarding medication, access to drugstores is not guaranteed: take along enough to last the tour. Similarly, though tour coaches are required to have federally-inspected first aid kits aboard, don't take it for granted that stocks of aspirin, bandages, and other supplies are abundant. Finally, bring along a small ice chest if you need to keep your medication in a cool place.

The Tour Director and the Driver

The tour director (also known as the guide, escort, tour conductor, or tour manager) is the heart and soul of group travel. The majority of tour operators expect their guide to offer expert commentary and ensure that the clientele get the tour they bought in the brochure. Because the brochure is tantamount to a contract, any change in the intinerary, meal, and lodging arrangements should be explained by the director.

According to a 1985 survey by *Travel-Holiday* magazine, tour clientele regard the director as the most influential factor in determining the success of their trip. As such, companies take great care in their selection of guides. Less than a decade ago, this job was relegated to the province of teachers on vacation, college

Your tour director is the heart and soul of group travel.

students, and others one would expect to see in seasonal work. The domestic travel boom has changed that to some extent. Nowadays the better companies feature full-time professionals who possess the erudition and savoir-faire of their fabled European counterparts. In addition to displaying chapter and verse knowledge of an area, the tour director sets the tone for the entire trip. How well the people interact and how the schedule and procedural considerations flow are largely a function of the effectiveness of the director as an efficiency expert and a raconteur.

Hence, successful practitioners of the trade all exhibit a genuine caring for people and a diplomat's flair for communication. One tour company, echoing the traits ascribed by John Hancock to the signers of the Declaration of Independence, outlined the tour director's job qualifications thusly: "He or she must possess the wisdom of Solomon, the patience of Job, and the valor of David." Amen.

The other mainstay aboard the vehicle is, of course, the driver.

Greyhound's motto, "safe, reliable, courteous," only conveys part of the story. Keeping the windows clean and maintaining a cheery smile on those early morning departures are as much a part of the job as is driving. These "roads scholars" can wear other hats as well. Some companies call on them to give tour commentary and to coordinate scheduling, as well as for logistics and accounting. These driver/guides are especially common on shorter charters. Still other outfits prefer to employ local guides. In this case the tour operator's representative is usually referred to as an escort, serving primarily as a host and coordinator and leaving commentary to another person.

Browsing the Brochures

Let's shift from discussing conditions on board the vehicle over to the prime vehicle of information itself, the tour brochure. Tour brochures come in all shapes, sizes, and colors, each offering faraway places and sunshiny faces. But be not deceived by glitz and tinsel. Behind all the fancy verbiage and "high-viz" glossies of paradise are objective standards of comfort and dollar value by which to evaluate a package.

Asking the Right Questions

Prior to deciphering the fine print, question yourself about the kind of travel experience you want to have.

Some questions you might want to ask are, "Am I looking for a relaxing trip with lots of free time or a sightseeing whirlwind? A spare, no-expense junket or a budget tour? A one- or two-week trip? A no-meals-included package or a fully inclusive tour? A tour with lots of walking or a sedentary experience?"

Finally, ask yourself whether or not the destination of the tour is conducive to your overall preferences. The more you can define the limits and nature of the package before reading what's in the itinerary, the less vulnerable you'll be to sugarcoated brochure jargon. Remember, you are choosing the tour to fit your needs. Moreover, if you approach your tour with a clear set of goals, you'll be better able to take advantage of the services of a travel agent.

In addition to figuring out where to go, perhaps the most fundamental consideration is the duration of the trip. Two-week tours generally feature more two-night stops than their abbreviated counterparts. But remember, while a longer trip might offer more leisure, it can also expose you to the rigors of extended travel. For many people, two weeks can be a long time to spend on a motor coach. By contrast, a shorter tour might lack the advantage of protracted stays in a locale, but there is less need to pace yourself during the trip. If you handle extended traveling well and the tour is well planned, other factors may take priority in choosing an itinerary.

In any case, do not calculate your time on the road on the basis of the number of days listed in the brochure. It's common practice for tour companies to include the days you spend going to or from the tour gateway (where the tour begins or ends) with the total days aboard the coach. Thus, when you're evaluating the pace of the tour, you can usually subtract a day or two from the total listed in the brochure.

The Travel Agent's Role in Choosing a Tour

While you are the only one who can ultimately decide what you want in a tour, a travel agent can facilitate this process in a number of ways. These professionals represent the interests of both the client and the tour operator. In much the same way an insurance broker is commissionable by an insurance carrier but at the same time assumes responsibilities on behalf of the client, a travel agent is the public's link to the tour industry. His or her responsibilities can include the placement of reservations, preparation of documentation, and most importantly, counseling.

Given the array of alternatives in price, service, and sightseeing options, professional advice can be especially beneficial to your decision-making process.

Many first-time tour travelers erroneously believe that agents are inclined to sell the tour that nets them the most generous commission. Fortunately, most travel agencies cannot operate successfully without repeat business, so it's unlikely you will be sold a tour just for the short-term profit on a commission. Furthermore, you can trust that any post-tour complaints against the tour operator will be given serious consideration by your agent. Agents want your continued patronage and are prepared to act as an advocate for your rights if there is a need for redress of grievances.

On occasion you may encounter a problem on tour that is the result of negligence by the agent. Perhaps a flight time at the tour's end is not logistically synchronized with the itinerary, or an agent's assurance of some special service is not satisfied. In these cases reputable professionals will gladly accept your collect call and help rectify the situation.

Assessing the Tour's Value

Commonly, first-time travelers determine a trip's value by calculating the per diem cost of a package—i.e., dividing the total price by the number of days of travel. Knowing the ratio of dollars per day is useful in determining the comparative cost of tours, but it tells you little about the value you are getting for your dollar. True value is determined by the quantity and quality of the meals, lodging, and sightseeing services provided by the package, in relation to what you're paying.

Meals

There is an old saying, "We can do without books, but we can't do without cooks." The same can be said about the importance of cuisine to the tour experience. Sampling Maine lobster, Alberta beef, and other indigenous fare is as great an attraction as New England fall foliage and the Canadian Rockies.

Meals are playing an increasingly important part in determining a tour's comparative value. Tauck Tours vice president Chuck Tauck regards meals as one of the most fundamental components in pricing a tour, stating, "In addition to being one of the special pleasures of tour travel, meals are rapidly becoming the most costly aspect of many fully-inclusive tours in the U.S. and Canada."

A look at menu prices in leading tour destinations makes it clear why the vast majority of tours does not offer all meals with carte blanche service. Prices for breakfast, lunch, and dinner, including tax and tip, can often exceed fifty dollars per person per day in resort environments. Thus, most tour companies opt to provide only some meals and/or restricted menu service. Since many folks are concerned with diet, this would seem an equitable way of keeping costs down. At the same time, a paucity of meals can cause considerable inconvenience and expense.

To further complicate matters, some brochures state "meals included," but do not specify how many of these meals are set menu and buffet and how many are table d'hôte service. As you can see, understanding the brochures in this regard is no simple matter.

Independent dining can be more expensive than meals included in the package, because restaurants make lower group rates available to tour operators. There's also something to be said for not having the task of finding a good place to eat after a hard day of sightseeing. The decision to have meals included or excluded comes down to your budget and dietary preferences.

If you have a special diet, inform the tour company. With the exception of kosher meals, there is usually no problem in getting what you want unless there are rigid, set menus.

One way to get a "fix" on your trip's culinary offerings is by checking the ratings of the hotels on the itinerary with the agent or in a Mobil or AAA guide. It's a safe bet that good hotel ratings reflect quality dining rooms. On many tours, you eat a majority of your meals in these establishments. Portion size varies, but chances are you'll encounter too much food, as opposed to too little. If hunger is ever a problem, most itineraries incorporate coffee breaks with rest stops. Then, too, you can always bring along a small snack to maintain your blood sugar.

Accommodations

A second dimension that comes into play when pricing a tour is the nature of the accommodations. To begin, you might want to research the locations of the listed hotels in order to assess their convenience to shopping or sightseeing. For example, if you are going to have a lot of free time in the cities you'll be visiting, you may prefer hotels that are centrally located. In the case of accommodations located in an area known for a particular landmark, the distance from that attraction, or the vantage point on it offered by the hotel, is of paramount importance.

It should also be mentioned that accommodations outside the center of a city are not necessarily undesirable. Indeed in such an area as a megalopolis in the Southwest, a resort on the urban periphery is often preferable. The downtowns of San Diego and Phoenix, for example, are far surpassed for attractiveness and comfort by their bordering resort towns of La Jolla and Scottsdale.

If you can't find out where you'll be staying from the tour operator's literature, the agent, or the tour company itself, caution is advised. A brochure without any of this information has great potential to deceive. Using adjectives like "deluxe" without any substantiation, and promising nothing more tangible than "first-class service," a tour company can cut corners without fear of reprisal.

Perhaps the most fundamental consideration related to accommodations is your bed specifications. Unless otherwise stated, most companies will book two separate beds in a room. As king-size beds are often in short supply, it's a good idea to arrange for them through your agent beforehand, rather than rely on your tour director to call each hotel ahead of time.

Single Travelers

A discussion of bed specifications would not be complete without references to single travelers. As most hotel rooms contain a pair of beds, tour companies book the majority of their accommodations on the basis of two to a room. The traveler who wants a room to his or her self is often assessed an extra charge to make up for the lost revenue. The charge can vary, but usually it represents 30- to 50-percent more than each member of a twosome would pay. To help singles cut costs, many tour operators offer a "booking to share option" where you are assigned a roommate. Not only does this save hundreds of dollars, but also it can get new friendships off to a rousing start.

The Importance of Sequencing

Something else to be aware of is the importance of sequencing—that is, the order in which the destinations come up during the tour. Since first and last impressions are enduring, you should pay particular attention to the itineraries on these days. Does the itinerary begin or end in a place where altitude and culture shock add to the stress and fatigue of joining or departing a tour? Are the destinations of the first part of the trip such that those of the last part will prove to be an anticlimax? How many long-mileage days are at the beginning, or the end, of the tour? Other queries pertinent to sequential logistics and pacing include: Do the two-night stops take advantage of a key destination and/or comfortable lodgings? Are there enough "breathers" in the itinerary to enable you to have enough energy to appreciate sightseeing meccas? Is there enough time?

Such questions are often hard to answer without the help of a good guidebook or a travel agent familiar with the terrain. To this end we offer a guide to the guidebooks. This listing also features selected travel magazines and videos. Supplement these resources with the destination material in Part II of this book.

Recommended Guidebooks

There is no frigate like a book to take us to lands far away.

—Emily Dickinson, 1856

Few of the current multitude of travel tomes are specifically geared to the interests of the tour traveler. With your creature comforts prearranged, you don't need the long list of hotels and restaurants offered in traditional guidebooks. Instead you are better served with background on the history, people, sightseeing highlights, and local color of a region.

The resources outlined below were chosen precisely because they focus on what many guidebooks often give short shrift: a sense of place. As a result, they can be indispensible in evaluating your itinerary and planning your trip.

Periodicals

The Sunday New York Times Travel Section

The "What's Doing" section gives a one-page rundown of a particular region or highlight. The essentials of sightseeing, customs, seasonal weather conditions and events, as well as other travel talk about an area, are set off in abbreviated captioned format. Elsewhere in the travel section, companion articles offer a more in-depth perspective on a compelling travel landmark or attraction.

National Geographic Traveler

The publication of articles often coincides with the best seasons to visit the areas being discussed. Color photos, lively commentary, and a breakdown of sites similar to the previously described *New York Times* travel section make *Traveler* excellent for choosing and planning a tour. It is published quarterly through the National Geographic Society, available by subscription only.

The National Geographic Society maps can be useful on many tours. Surprisingly, many domestic companies neglect to supply an adequate map, especially ones as detailed as these. A close look at a map beforehand can tell you something about vegetation, elevation, proximity of tour sites, and the pacing of the trip.

To this end, a new publication of the National Geographic Society is recommended. *Close-Up U.S.A.* collates all sixteen of the society's maps, annotated with sightseeing highlights. In addition, a "mile-o-meter" makes it possible to calculate the distances between tour venues. These publications may be obtained by writing The National Geographic, P.O. Box 1640, Washington, D.C. 20007.

Travel Holiday

Travel Holiday's annual reader's poll honors those tour companies, cruise lines, and hotel chains that are ranked at the top by the respondents to the magazine's survey. The most common concerns and complaints of the tour traveler are discussed.

The "Travel Advisor" section also offers practical tips on everything from airline fares to hotel phones. *Travel Holiday* is available monthly, at newsstands as well as by subscription. Address: *Travel-Holiday* Magazine, Travel Building, 51 Atlantic Avenue, Floral Park, New York 11001.

Tours!

Tours! is published by the National Tour Association, whose membership includes tour operators, restauranteurs, innkeepers, gift shop owners, state tourism promoters and concessionaires. *Tours!* serves as a vehicle to get information about

North American destinations out to the public. In the format of an "in-flight" magazine, it includes lively destination pieces on the leading tour venues. A "Tour Tips" section gives advice on how to have a *bon voyage*. This highly informative magazine is published in each of the four seasons and distributed by NTA member-tour companies to their clientele.

AARP Brochures

The American Association of Retired People is a nonprofit umbrella organization that includes an insurance group, a tour company, a book publisher, and a magazine to serve the needs of senior citizens. Their complete service orientation is reflected in their brochures. Not satisfied with just the tedious price breakdowns and words-with-a-smile travel copy, these publications actually prepare the traveler in the manner of a concise and comprehensive guidebook.

Detailed descriptions of the topography and the stories behind the scenery offer insights into many of the "must-see" destinations. As of this writing, the first three of these brochures are free upon request from AARP. Thereafter there is a nominal fee, unless of course you find an agent with AARP's literature in stock. Address: AARP Travel Service, 4801 West 110th Street, Overland Park, Kansas 66211. Phone: 1-800-448-7010 (in Kansas call collect 913-345-0404).

Tours and Resorts

This magazine features a tour, a city, and a resort of the month. Each is feted with an article that includes the names, addresses, and phone numbers of tour companies that run charters encompassing the resorts and destinations discussed in the text. *Tours and Resorts* is published bimonthly and is available at some newsstands or by subscription at P.O. Box 3299, Harlan, Iowa 51537.

Guidebooks

Insight Guides

These handsome Prentice-Hall publications are a cross between a coffee-table book and a guidebook. They begin with in-depth information on the history, people, and geology of a locale. This is followed by a breakdown of popular touring corridors within the area, written by local travel writers. Regional flavor is emphasized more than a detailed description of every milepost along the road.

Moreover, *Insight's* roadside observations pull no punches, a contrast to the upbeat-at-all-costs tone of most books in this genre. Best of all, the pages are adorned with dozens of spectacular color photos and maps. Often there are additional sections focusing on special interests such as photography, wildlife, or folk art.

The only fault the tour traveler might find with these books is that they can be too bulky to fit in hand luggage. No matter. You will not find a better guidebook for the tour traveler. Current domestic titles include *Alaska, Canada, Northern California, Southern California, The Rockies, The Southwest, The Pacific Northwest, New York State, New England, Florida* and the all-inclusive *Crossing the U.S.A.*

Consumer Guide to Packaged Travel

Before visiting your travel agent, you might want to skim this book published by Globe Pecquot Press. The listing of domestic companies, and one or two paragraphs describing their offerings, provides a good overview of what's available. While this same kind of information can be culled from your agent, *Consumer Guide* enables you to survey more quickly the range of tours offered by dozens of companies. Before this listing, a "how-to" section devoted to preparing you for the journey is included.

Because this procedural information also addresses foreign travel and cruises, this section dilutes the focus away from domestic bus tour packages. Nevertheless, the book is a veritable encyclopedia of tour travel options in North America.

Videos

Recently, videos on leading tour destinations have been independently produced in cooperation with tour operators. They are marketed directly through the operator or through travel magazines.

Obviously, you should purchase the video that most closely conforms to the itinerary of the tour you plan to take. As of this writing, availability of these videos is still confined to a handful of tour operators. If your tour of choice is not so blessed, I recommend a company called Vacations on Video. They produce videos for several leading tour operators and cruise lines. Even if you are not a client of these organizations, chances are that any of the Vacations on Video series will give you a notion of what it's like to "do" a particular region within the context of a tour. This tends to be better than the garden-variety travel video that focuses on a particular destination with no regard for the parameters of tour travel. For more information, write Vacations on Video, 1309 East Northern, Phoenix, Arizona 85020.

Contracts: The Fine Print on the Back Page

You know where you want to go. You've read a number of brochures and a few guidebooks about the chosen destination. You've evaluated and compared itineraries and meals/lodging. All that's left to cover in the final decision-making process is whatever is in the fine print.

The fine print that outlines the contractual obligation between client and tour operator is often relegated to the back page, printed in small type, and written in technical "travelese." Such a format makes it easy for you to skip over important details. An agent might help glean the essentials, but ultimately it behooves you to pay attention!

What's included in the fine print? For starters, basic information on how to book, the amount of deposit required, final payment dates, how refunds will be handled, cancellation charges, and various matters related to the operation and management of the tour. In addition to being a source to form expectations of the trip, the information can serve as a vehicle for redress of grievances. To these ends, familiarize yourself with the following components of the fine print:

- ☐ Reservation and payment policy
- ☐ Refund and cancellation policy
- ☐ Transfers (e.g., transportation upon joining and departing a tour)
- ☐ Taxes, tips, entrance fees, and other charges
- ☐ Details about the administration of sightseeing service (e.g., local guide, tour manager, escort, etc.)
- ☐ Baggage limitations and insurance
- ☐ Health and documentation
- ☐ Warnings about health hazards
- ☐ Information regarding possible changes on price, carrier, hotel, etc.
- ☐ Any limitation of tour operator's responsibility

Occasionally the following optional directives are included:

- ☐ Tour capacity and minimum number of participants
- ☐ Approximate travel times between destinations
- ☐ Smoking and seat rotation policies
- ☐ Restrictions on children
- ☐ Bed configuration specifications
- ☐ Booking to share and other concerns of the single traveler

(These recommendations courtesy of the U.S.T.O.A.)

Refund and Cancellation Policies

Cancellation deadlines for refunds vary greatly, as do policies regarding reimbursement for cutting a trip short. Regardless of how you feel about the clause in your particular brochure, it probably won't affect your choice of tour package. After all, how many of us begin a tour with the expectation of having to cancel?

However, the unexpected has been known to happen. Missing a tour is bad enough. Why compound it with a penalty fee for cancellation? Spare yourself such unpleasant surprises. Take note if full or partial refunds are granted for cancellation due to sickness, injury, hospitalization, or death in the family. Then check the deadline for notification. At this point you will be in a position to decide if trip cancellation insurance is a wise investment. It can be purchased from your travel agent or from many leading operators, who sometimes offer optional coverage at a good buy.

You should also be concerned about protection from another kind of unforeseen development. According to a 1987 House subcommittee hearing, complaints about travel fraud are among the top ten problems confronted by consumer protection agencies and law enforcement officials. A common scam is to declare bankruptcy and abscond with client deposits, or just disappear with the money. Of course such practices are restricted to "fly-by-nights" on the fringe of the industry. Many of these fast-buck artists entered the field with the 1982 deregulation of the airline industry. You can avoid them by seeking out tour operators who belong to either National Tour Association (NTA) or U.S. Tour Operator's Association (USTOA).

These industry trade associations together with American Society of Travel Agents (ASTA) insure deposits and are able to refund your money in the event of bankruptcy. Consider the consumer protection program of the largest organization for domestic tour operators, NTA, which takes effect in 1988. Each of the 500 member companies is now covered for an amount of up to $100,000 dollars of deposits. ASTA and USTOA plans are comparable.

If your tour company is a member of any of these agencies, your confidence is justified. They can also be trusted to follow through on other claims in their brochures, or else they would lose their good standing in the professional community. If you don't see the logo of one of these trade groups in the brochure, check with your travel agent about the company's status.

The Question of Tips

Another section of the "back page" that is too often glossed over focuses on gratuities. While tips are often a small percentage of the total tour price, they nonetheless are an important—and problematic—enough subject to warrant comment.

Important because most of us want to do the right thing and acknowledge superior service with a fitting personal gesture; problematic because the straight 15-to-20-percent formula for restaurant meals doesn't apply to sightseeing services. Consequently you may be unsure how to tip a driver or a guide. Although recommended ranges are set down by many companies, as the tour nears a climax you're still likely to hear considerable debate about tipping etiquette. Here are a couple of tips on tips.

Package tours most often include gratuities for dining room meal service and luggage assistance at hotels on the itinerary. On the other hand, you are usually responsible for tipping bartenders and chambermaids. Apply the same standard as you would for traveling independently. This is generally 15 percent gratuity for drinks and $1.50 per room for housekeeping services.

As for your tour director and driver, your best guideline is the range set down in your tour operator's literature. Regarding this suggested gratuity, keep in perspective what these sightseeing functionaries do for their money. Among other things, the driver and/or tour director provide driving and tour commentary, confirmation and coordination of luggage handling, lodging and meals, group dynamics and stress management, accounting, routing logistics, as well as such optional courtesies as removing hand luggage from overhead racks and helping clients off the coach.

Frequently the tipping mistake involves the phrase "per person per day." This statement does not just refer to the member of the couple who has the responsibility of making the gesture. A fair tip should reflect services accorded to two people.

Finally, gratuities are best extended privately, befitting a gesture of personal gratitude. In other words, no group collections! Passing the hat is impersonal and crude. Handing an envelope with a note to your driver or guide just prior to saying good-bye is the proper way to dignify your appreciation.

Baggage Limitations and Insurance

Most fully inclusive tours limit one bag per person. This is because people tend to bring more than they need and the surfeit of suitcases would translate into exorbitant bellman gratuities.

The major reason for limiting baggage, however, is space. The "bay" of even the most spacious motor coach cannot comfortably hold much more than sixty average-size suitcases. As such, most tours include a luggage gratuity for one case and charge extra for each additional piece. This fee is usually derived by multiplying the number of hotels by an average gratuity: a dollar "in" and a dollar "out."

A related concern is suitcase damage. Most tour companies disavow any responsibility for this unfortunate occurrence because liability is so difficult to determine. You may receive some form of recompense through reporting the damage to the tour operator's representative, provided that person can act as an advocate with the offending hotel or airline. The latter are heavily insured and are generally able and willing to cover repair costs if it's clear that the damage came from their mishandling. However, do not expect compensation for damage due to what may be termed "life of the garment."

Most travel agents and some tour operators sell luggage insurance. This is especially recommended if your case is borrowed or has great sentimental value. Generally, proper packing and sturdy luggage are sufficient insurance against battered bags. Detailed recommendations about suitcase styles and packing procedures appear in the next chapter.

In addition to being charged for extra luggage, you might be expected to pay for transfers. This means that upon joining or departing a tour, the costs attendant to getting to or from the airport and hotel may be borne in part by yourself. This policy is necessitated by the wide disparity of arrival and departure times rendering a group pickup/drop by tour coach impractical. In large cities, you can expect cab fare to be quite costly—have sufficient cash on hand.

Limitation of the Tour Operator's Liability

The legal limits of tour operator responsibility are further defined by a proviso covering changes in hotel and price. Reasons for such fluctuations and substitutions are mostly due to seasonal considerations of supply and demand. Brochures featuring national park hotels include information that is subject to these changes. The Chateau Lake Louise, the Banff Springs Hotel, the Ahwahnee in Yosemite Park, and the Jasper Park Lodge in the Canadian Rockies, for example, have significant rate changes conforming to peak and off-peak seasons. In other instances, these hotels must be dropped from an itinerary when no rooms are available. Many other heavily touristed "non-park" areas such as Victoria, British Columbia, and Williamsburg, Virginia, also experience significant seasonal changes in price and/or limitations on the availability of lodging.

While the tour company can document these potential changes in its brochure, it cannot anticipate supplier errors due to overbooking. In the case when a tour is "walked" from a listed hotel, the tour operator is generally absolved of responsibility. The same principle applies to restaurant and sightseeing services. On these rare occasions where cancellations occur, the hotel, restaurant, or concessionaire usually arranges a refund or a substitution of comparable quality. In this way they uphold a good working relationship with the tour operator, and try to merit future patronage.

The tour operator is similarly exempt from blame when some alteration in the itinerary and/or services listed in the brochure is due to an "act of God," rebellion, strike, or happenstance outside the control of the company. The legal term describing this is "force majeure." Consider the rock slides that sometimes block that portion of California Highway 1 known as Big Sur. Although the tour operator cannot be held legally responsible for this, it's only good business for the company to make every reasonable effort to achieve equitable tour modifications. As such, many carriers who are not able to complete the entire Big Sur route temper their clients' disappointment by going partway along this scenic coastal drive and then turning around.

CHAPTER 2

My Travel Agent Never Told Me

Sunrise at Lake Louise . . . touching the crack in the Liberty Bell . . . jambalaya and jazz at Sunday brunch in New Orleans—on the eve of a tour, such travel fantasies fill your dreams. As the clock winds down, you'll find yourself looking in the newspaper each day for weather forecasts specific to your itinerary and trying to figure out the appropriate dress for your journey. By the time your suitcase is out of the closet, chances are you'll have come to quite a few conclusions about packing, health, photography, and other practical travel concerns. Here are some tour tips culled from experience to aid in pretrip preparations.

Packing Precautions

If there's any truism that applies to all tour travelers, it's that we usually pack more than is necessary. Although the following list of recommendations might not change this venerated art of suitcase-stuffing, it will help identify things you "shouldn't leave home without."

First, some precautionary measures. To avoid having your film faded or erased by the X-rays of airline security machines, put it in lead-lined pouches available at a camera store. Despite assurances to the contrary from airline security personnel, it takes no more than five exposures of this sort to cause serious damage to film. Should security guards be amenable to hand-searching film in a sealed plastic bag, even better.

Reserve space in your hand luggage for a sweater to counteract the "over-amped" air-conditioning common to airline cabins and tour buses. Here's where to stash your tour documents, valuables, and medication. If you become separated from your larger suitcases, you'll appreciate having objects of value in your hand luggage. This practice spares you potential losses or inconvenience. Remember, also, to take some extra stamps, as post offices tend to be in short supply in many tour locales.

Sturdy luggage secured by a latch is recommended in lieu of cloth/vinyl zipper bags, which are more apt to give way over time. Aluminum cases made by Zero Halliburton have a lifetime guarantee, and despite the price (which can exceed two hundred dollars), they are a good value for those who travel a lot. Perhaps such an investment can be put in perspective by a look into your luggage graveyard—the closet or attic where the remains of suitcases lie: broken handles, split zippers, and ruptured sides.

Whatever your feelings about expense, leave behind lightweight soft-side luggage that might be preferable when you carry your own bags. A hard-sided suitcase can withstand the wear and tear of other bags atop it on a luggage cart. Another advantage is greater resistance to mildew in the aftermath of a downpour. And perhaps more important, hardcases don't expand, so overpacking is prevented.

Tape a copy of your itinerary to the inside of your suitcase. This will speed its return to you if it is left behind.

Suitcase Stuffing

Even if your film, your valuables, and your bags manage to emerge unscathed from your travels, it's a safe bet you'll have to do battle with the number one enemy for those who live out of a suitcase: wrinkles. Here are some popular ways of combatting the major curse of the suitcase-stuffer.

- ☐ Most preventative measures involve compartmentalizing your luggage in such a way that the act of extracting one item will not disorganize the whole bag. Common methods include plain and seal-top plastic bags.
- ☐ A light wool sweater-vest and other pullovers that don't show wrinkles can hide a multitude of sins.
- ☐ Steam from the shower in your bathroom can work wonders, particularly on clothing of lightweight material.
- ☐ Some knits do not withstand wrinkles. To test a knit garment, gather a good handful and squeeze hard. If the knit shows wrinkles, that's how the garment will look after a day of traveling.
- ☐ Don't severely underpack or overpack your suitcase. Garments moving around in a loosely packed case or a jumble of clothes pressed together will result in that "slept-in" look.
- ☐ Place infrequently used items on the bottom. Having pants and/or skirts in the middle and shirts or sweaters on top might be an efficient method of organization.
- ☐ There are many different ways of folding items to minimize wrinkles. By the time most folks get around to taking this kind of trip, they usually have their own system. Rather than belabor the varied and intricate nuances of suitcase stuffing, we refer neophyte packers to a free pamphlet on the subject *Getting a Handle on Luggage*, Samsonite Traveler Advisory Service, P.O. Box 38300 Dept. 20, Denver, Colorado 80238.

There is one method, however, that deserves special notice, particularly if you have a larger suitcase. Begin by placing shirts and blouses on hangers. Cover four or five with the kind of bag available from commercial dry cleaners, fold in half and pack, hangers and all. Not only does this prevent wrinkles, but it can spare you the ordeal of hotel hangers, which come in parts and require considerable sleight of hand to manipulate. Just remember to put paper or masking tape around the sharp wire edges to keep your clothes from being impaled.

As many of you might already have soft-side cases, it behooves me to pass on some pertinent advice. Unlike hard-side luggage, Cordura bags and other flexible totes should be packed to capacity; any play in the fabric and it can get caught between the other cases and be pinched. By contrast, a sturdier case with no give can't sustain the tension of being forced shut over time. Sooner or later, the lock will break or the rivets will give way; so leave some breathing room. For more information on packing a fabric case, send your request for a free pamphlet on the subject with a self-addressed stamped envelope to: *How To Pack Brochure*, Cordura Fibers Marketing Center, Center Road Building, Wilmington, Delaware 19898.

Living Out of a Suitcase

When you are on tour, you will often find that there is not time to fully unpack your belongings. Thus, it's important to organize your suitcase so that it can serve as a closet and a drawer. By packing and unpacking a few times at home, you'll be able to judge the efficiency of your system.

From a Tour Director's Notebook

The following entries from a tour director's notebook come courtesy of the hindsight that, according to the sages, makes geniuses of us all.

Photos, Radios, and Phones

For best results when taking pictures from inside a coach window be sure to place your camera near but not touching the glass. This cuts the glare and takes advantage of the polarized glass on most bus windows. It's also important to adjust your shutter speed to compensate for the movement of the coach; 1/25th of a second faster will usually accommodate the speed of the vehicle.

A transistor radio with headset can prove surprisingly valuable on tour. Whether you want the music to make a stretch of dead road go by faster or to create your own quiet time in preference to tour commentary, just plug in the headphones. Quite a few hotels do not have radios in the room (particularly national park hotels, many of which also have government prohibitions on television), so for that convenience you might want to pack your own.

Long-distance calls on hotel phones are quite costly, with surcharges up to 30 percent. Telephone credit cards, calling your party collect with the understanding that they call you back, and pay phones are essential to cut costs. You should also be aware that many hotel phone systems don't give preferential rates for calls made during "off-peak" hours. It has also become common practice for many big city hotels to charge a dollar for local calls.

Great and Not-So-Great Expectations

Tours that include special events such as the world's fair or the Olympics should be approached with realistic expectations—namely that the event is an additional highlight, not the focal point of a tour.

Earthquakes, despite being an ever-present danger in California and Alaska, need not discourage you from going to these popular destinations. The October '87 Los Angeles earthquake offers a case in point. Despite a quake of high magnitude and subsequent aftershocks, only six casualties were recorded within the affected population area of 20 million. It was the media that gave the situation overtones of Armageddon. If you added up the amount of quake-related deaths in California for the past fifty years, it wouldn't begin to approximate the annual total from auto accidents in the metropolitan areas of the major American cities. Whatever, the safest place to be if you're indoors during a tremor is under a doorway.

On tours that feature meals in a hotel dining room prepare yourself for instances of slow service. In certain parts of the country, a more relaxed pace is adopted. Such areas include the western and southern regions of the U.S., all national parks, and much of Canada. If you must eat and run, mention this at the start to the person serving you. In general you can expedite service by sitting in small parties (to make it easier for all orders to be brought out at once) and placing your order prior to going off to the restroom.

If it's clear that the slowness of the service cannot be rationalized as "fine dining," then summon your tour director if possible. Quality companies usually have enough rapport with an establishment to ensure that your problems get taken to the top. Whatever you do, don't bring up slow service or any other complaint to your tour director when there is no longer an opportunity to rectify the situation. Your interests will be better served after the fact by a comment card to the tour company or establishment in question.

Although weather and wardrobe will be treated more specifically in the chapters to follow, a good rule of thumb is "dress like an onion, ready to peel." By dressing in layers you can adjust to the diverse climatic conditions encountered during the course of a typical day. Be sure you have walking shoes that are well broken-in! The temptation to buy a new pair of shoes for the trip is understandable but not well-advised. You're better off buying them long before you leave to get them comfortable ahead of time.

To get a read-out beforehand on the weather conditions in a particular area, two good sources are:

1. *The Times Books—The World Weather Guide*, by E.A. Pearce and C.G. Smith, published by New York Times Book Company, 1984. The mailing address is 130 Fifth Avenue, New York, New York 10011. The book contains a section-by-section breakdown of the nation's climate belts with average temperatures, rainfall, etc., as well as idiosyncrasies of regional weather.
2. Banana Republic Weather Report—1-800-325-7270. This toll-free number is maintained by a travel-safari clothing outfitter and purveyor of travel books and maps. Travel advisories include up-to-the-minute read-outs on temperature, fog conditions, and miscellaneous advice on a particular locale.

Canada

Despite superficial similarities to the U.S., Canada has some very distinct customs. Acknowledging these differences will smooth out your journey north of the border.

Although American currency is usually accepted in Canada, you will want to exchange some money beforehand. Money exchanges should always be done in a bank to get the best rate.

Be prepared to encounter an English atmosphere in the west and a pervasive French influence to the east. Also, expect to see a coat and tie worn to dinner throughout Canada, even in places that would warrant casual dress in the U.S.

Despite this superficial formality, you'll find urban Canadians just as friendly as their small-town counterparts. This is not always an easy task. Outnumbered ten to one across a border spanning five time zones, Canadians agonize over how to be good friends with their superpower neighbor and still preserve their culture and identity. It helps for Americans to refrain from complaining that things are not exactly the way they are back home.

Despite Canada's rugged outdoor image, 80 percent of its 25.3-million population huddles within one hundred miles of the U.S. border. Sixty percent of these people reside in the east, leaving the prairies, the far north, and the western parts of the country the sight of some long bus rides.

In lieu of collective bargaining as it is practiced in the states, strikes are undertaken not as a last resort but as a matter of course. Work stoppages by ports, railroads, the post office, air carriers and other essential services are frequent. They seem to target peak visitation times, so stay informed.

The Canadian postal system is notoriously slow, especially in the sparsely populated west. Use it only if you must!

Across the country, Canadian beer and apple cider are excellent. However, you cannot take either an open bottle or more than a liter of alcohol back to the U.S. Coach tours usually pass more easily through customs and immigration than the independent traveler does. The list of what is considered contraband continually changes, so be sure to check U.S. customs. (A pamphlet *Know Before You Go* is available from most travel agents.) Incidentally, Hudson Bay and Eatons are retailers found around the country who stock indigenous specialities such as furs and jade at a good price.

Finally, concerning border crossings, citizens of the United States can cross the Canadian border in either direction without passports or visas. You must bring proof of citizenship, however, such as a passport or birth certificate. A driver's license or voter's registration card is not usually accepted as proof of citizenship. If you spend more than forty-eight hours in Canada and wish to purchase gifts, you may return with up to $400 worth of merchandise for personal or household use without paying duty.

And Finally . . .

After many miles looking out the front windshield at vistas ranging from Mt. McKinley to Monticello, it is my firm conviction that 90 percent of the success of a tour is contingent upon the people on it. As I tell groups at the beginning of each tour:

Life is like a journey taken on a train,
With each one of us seated by a window pane

I might sit beside you or on the other side,
But let's be pleasant to each other,
It's so short a ride.

Trite perhaps, but the meaning of this verse is as true off the coach as it is when you're on board.

CHAPTER 3

Out of the Armchair and Onto the Road

Having documented the nuts and bolts aspects of motor coach touring, let's simulate an interlude from an actual tour. First, meet two of our tour companions, Mr. and Mrs. E.Z. Ryder from Eastern Seaboard, New Jersey. Prior to this tour, they traveled mostly during summers or on sabbatical from their jobs teaching at a local college. Usually the purpose of their trips was study and research. This trip is designed to celebrate their freedom from work-related travel and, of course, their jobs.

Recently retired, they finally have the chance to see northern California and the Northwest the way they always wanted to—at leisure. Money is less of a consideration than in the past. However, when their agent stated the price of the tour they wanted, they couldn't quite suppress a look that said, "Do you still want to go through with this, dear?" Understanding their misgivings, the agent reassured them by outlining the costs of the more expensive meals/lodging components of the tour if done independently. He also pointed out that the tour company the Ryders chose was more expensive than its counterparts in the region. The higher rate, he said, was for a good reason: as a long-established and reputable tour operator, it could be counted on to fulfill the arrangements stated in the brochure.

Ultimately the Ryders are sold on the package when the agent says, "With tours, as in so many situations, it's the little things we remember. You might go to enjoy such Northwest attractions as the Space Needle and Mt. St. Helens, but chances are you'll remember most fondly the experiences you haven't anticipated. For instance, this itinerary features a little Mom and Pop place on the Rogue River that serves freshly-caught salmon. Before cooking it, Pop sometimes brings you the fish to see while it's still wriggling in the net. For dessert, there is pie with blackberries picked that morning. After lunch, you hop into a mail boat that, in addition to being a postal carrier for folks on the river, is your magic carpet into the wilds of Oregon. This is just one of the intimate perspectives on the region that this company is famous for," he concluded.

And so, with visions of the great Northwest dancing in their heads, the E.Z. Ryders flew to the tour gateway, San Francisco. Having never been to San Francisco, the intrepid travelers came two days early and booked a room at a reduced rate arranged by the tour operator. After a day of independent sightseeing, they joined the group and tour director, a handsome college student named Brian Long. In a speech over dinner in the banquet room of the motel, Brian, himself a native of the Northwest, prepared the group for the next two weeks of adventure.

"You're about to head into a region renowned for its beautiful landscape and livability. There are quite a few once-in-a-lifetime experiences here, so every morning we'll rise early to take in as much as we can. Am I correct in assuming that you've come to see the Northwest and that you can sleep when you get home?"

The question is greeted by applause from everyone in the room except the Ryders. Since retirement they have become late-risers and the prospect of early morning reveille is not cause for joy. They brighten at the director's next comment, however.

"The tour is paced in such a way that we do the most ambitious days of travel at the beginning. After touring San Francisco tomorrow, for instance, we drive 300 miles up the Redwood Highway through the wine country to Eureka, California. By contrast, our last days are relaxing, low-mileage affairs conforming to the pace you'll be moving at towards the end of the tour.

"Getting back to our first day's schedule, because of union regulations and the specialized nature of touring San Francisco, we'll be having a local guide tomorrow. The tour starts at nine o'clock from the front door. Breakfast is on your own. Outside of this dinner, we don't provide meals in San Francisco, since there is no dearth of restaurant choices in and around the hotel. Moreover, just to limit you to the dining room here would inhibit your appreciation of the seafood and ethnic cuisine for which this city is famous.

"Before leaving tonight pick up the folder on restaurants, shopping, and independent sightseeing suggestions I've left at the door. Tomorrow's tour takes in Twin Peaks, Golden Gate Park, Chinatown, and all the other highlights described in the brochure. The whole itinerary takes three hours if you go back with us to the hotel on the bus. Some of you might take advantage of the option to return to the hotel by cable car from Fisherman's Wharf, our second-to-last stop.

"On the following day, we'll meet at the same place again at nine o'clock. After cool weather in the morning, you'll have temperatures in the eighties until we come to the redwoods after lunch. From then on, expect ten to fifteen degrees less. At day's end we're near the coast and a sweater will probably be necessary.

"There'll be a lot of walking today and tomorrow for those so inclined. If there aren't any questions, I'd now like to get to the major business of a get-acquainted banquet. When I call your name, raise your hand and tell the group where you're from. If you want, you might also tell us something about yourself and what you've come here to see."

As the group members proceed to introduce themselves, the

Ryders observe that except for the fact that most of the people are retired and from the East and the South, the group is quite diverse. But even as they speak of varied backgrounds, professions, and reasons for coming, the good will and gung-ho attitude in the room leaves little doubt that this group will be fun to travel with and easy to get to know.

The Ryders' intuitions are borne out the next day in the hotel coffee shop, but the conversation and friendliness don't stop at breakfast. During the day's sightseeing, the Ryders are asked both to pose in a picture for the people across the aisle and to join several couples for dinner.

After a full day taking in the hills and valleys of America's most romantic port-of-call, the Ryders return to their room early to prepare for the next day. The director requested that luggage be left just outside the door to be picked up by the bellman an hour before each morning departure. As such, the Ryders enact a routine they will repeat for the next two weeks. After setting aside clothes for the next day, they put their bags by the door to be close by the pick-up point on the morrow. A quick review of the brochure, a good-night kiss, and soon these erstwhile tour companions are off in dreamland.

A Day in the Life of a Tour

Although the wake-up call from the hotel operator the next morning comes as an unaccustomed shock, the couple soon fly into action as though they have been touring all their lives. They tend to personal needs in fifteen minutes, then review a checklist of the director's recommendations for the day. After making sure to have sunglasses, binoculars, and walking shoes ready, their thoughts turn to shopping opportunities mentioned by Brian. Between California wine and redwood souvenirs, they could probably take care of the children and the grandchildren in one day of shopping. They also note the director's recommendation to eat lightly, since lunch today will consist of hearty fare at a relatively early hour.

At the appointed time, the Ryders head out to board the bus, coffee and croissant in hand. They look at the seating chart tacked to the side of the door; for the sake of convenience, the director has devised an arbitrary seating arrangement for the first day. After lunch the tour will rotate clockwise from their assigned seat, the driver's side moving up two seats and the door side moving back. It happens that the Ryders will be near the high front windshield in the afternoon, a bonus for sightseeing in the redwoods.

As the rest of the group files on the coach, "I left my heart in San Francisco" plays on the tape deck, a fitting—if corny—farewell to their time in the city. Soon they are zigzagging through the hills towards the Golden Gate Bridge with the cliffside grandeur surrounding the San Francisco Bay spread out before them. Their gaze shifts from the panorama to Brian, who is about to set the stage for their journey along Highway 101. Before listening to his first words, let's take a moment to examine the importance of commentary to the motor coach tour experience, an art that goes back to antiquity.

Tour Talk

In many countries of the world, being a guide is a venerable profession. From the Louvre in Paris to the temples of Kyoto, these modern-day bards have shaped the perceptions of millions of world travelers. In recent decades, tour guides have become established on this continent, but with a difference. Without the age-old European or Asian cultural traditions in music and art, the American tour guide, particularly in the West, is more apt to wax poetic about the majestic landscape. After all, it is this nature on a grand scale that distinguishes us as a country. The national park idea was born in America, and our roadsides abound with such wonders as autumn in New England and the redwoods of California. By way of example, we are pleased to share with you comments on the touring route from San Francisco up through the wine country to the redwoods via U.S. Route 101.

Let's now return to our tour director, Brian Long, whose overview of the day begins with the following words:

"It's time to say good morning and good-bye. In a few minutes we'll be on the other side of the bridge that symbolizes San Francisco. The Golden Gate is also perhaps the foremost architectural landmark in the West, so it's altogether fitting that we save the most evocative landmark of this city for last.

"Poetic justice will come once again at day's end in the shadow of the oldest, largest living things known to humankind, the redwoods. In between we'll toast our good fortune at a Sonoma Valley Winery, where we've planned luncheon and a tour. For now, let's look back on our indelible memories of San Francisco. Whether it's the smell of sourdough and salt air coming in with the fog or sore feet from window-shopping at the wharf, I'm sure you'll agree the city has a way of staying with you. In a short while, we'll stop to look back across the bay at the San Francisco skyline and take a picture to remember her by."

As the director continues on about a Mt. St. Helens helicopter-flight option of limited interest to the Ryders, they gaze upon a stunning tableau of San Francisco Bay. The precipitous and circuitous road above Sausalito, an artist colony built into the hillside, enhance the couple's appreciation of letting "George, the driver, do it." If E.Z. were driving himself, his eyes would be glued to the road instead of the sailboats below. What's more, sitting high up in a motor coach affords the couple a greater field of vision than their car.

The director's voice suddenly reclaims the Ryders' attention. They will be coming to an overlook from which they can look back on the bridge, the bay, and the city skyline. As the bus pulls to a stop, the Ryders step out to see the vast view of the San Francisco Bay.

Aside from describing the magnificence of the landscape, the tour director also provides running commentary on the history and local color of each region. Brian now begins his introduction to the Redwood Highway that is to be their home for the day.

The Redwood Highway—
Land of Giant Trees and Chablis

"During the period between 1769 and 1821, Route 101 began as a yellow-blossomed footpath that followed the wild mustard planted by the missionaries. Because the line of twenty-one missions built by the padres came to an end north of San Francisco, highway planners decided to base the remainder of 101's routing on another quintessential California theme—the redwoods. That this Redwood Highway also passes through Sonoma County where American viniculture began reinforces the impression that 101 north of San Francisco is a path of living history. For this reason, the Redwood Highway is the choice route of the majority of tours heading north to Oregon.

"From the moment you arrive on the Redwood Highway after crossing the Golden Gate bridge, the cosmopolitan charm of San Francisco gives way to the cliffside artist community of Sausalito overlooking the San Francisco Bay. The air is fresher and cooler, and the sight of sailing craft and houseboats below rows of villas on terraced hillsides evokes the Mediterranean.

"As you head north, the landscape becomes increasingly rural, with the last vestiges of urban culture visible in San Rafael. As in San Francisco, the new blends with the old, exemplified by the bell tower of the old mission coexisting with the space-age contours of Frank Lloyd Wright's Marin County Civic Center. Not long after passing the coastal range's highest peak, Mount Tamalpais (2,578 feet), the road heads north to Sonoma County, home of botanist Luther Burbank, authors Jack London and Robert Louis Stevenson, as well as the cartoonist Charles "Peanuts" Schulz. Sonoma also contains historical landmarks, such as the battle site where California won independence from Mexico. Last but not least, it was the place where California popped the cork on her wine industry in 1857.

"Grape stakes, Bartlett pear orchards, and citrus groves can be seen as you continue to Cloverdale, the furthest point north where oranges are commercially grown. As you cross the Russian River north of town, the countryside becomes hillier and conifers begin to appear with the oak.

"The name Russian River bespeaks that nationality's presence in northern California. The Russian trappers' desire for fur pelts to trade for opium and tea in China prompted an incursion in the mid-eighteenth century. Modern occupants of the region range from marijuana growers and commune members to the captains of American politics and industry. The latter frolic each summer in their private Mendocino enclave, Bohemia Redwood Grove."

After delivering this long discourse, the director reassures

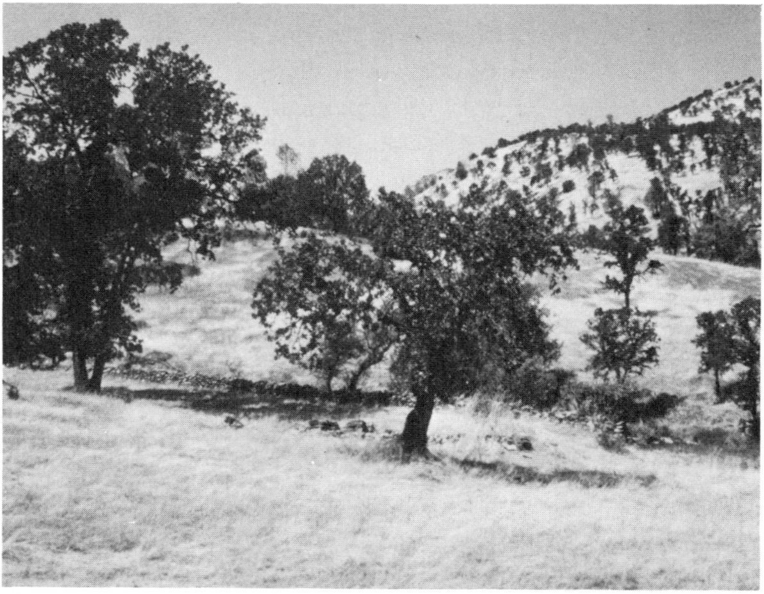

Parched hillsides inspired California's nickname, "The Golden State."

those in the group who might have found his rapid-fire commentary intrusive.

"Folks, forgive me for sounding a bit like an auctioneer at this juncture. But I prefer to err on the side of giving you too much background commentary at this point than too little. If I get it all out of the way now, you'll be better able to lie back and enjoy the duration of the tour. From here on, I'll be deferring more to the beauties of our surroundings and letting the scenery do the talking."

As the day unfolds, the group comes to appreciate their leader, who orchestrates the scenic drive through the wine country with Beethoven's "Pastorale" on the tape deck. In similar fashion, the director has the good sense to limit his commentary when words would only distract from the glory of the redwoods. As lunch draws near, Brian explains a bit more about procedure.

"After lunch we rotate two seats. Just remember S.O.S.—skip one and sit. Also keep in mind that a rest stop is planned up the road about forty minutes from now."

Company policies governing lost items and meals are taken up now. Alcoholic beverages are excluded from the tab picked up by the company on included meals. Hotels will send items left behind to the person's home address, as opposed to forwarding them to a hotel up the line.

For many in the group, lunchtime is a welcome respite from the unaccustomed sitting. Prior to lunch, a tour of the winery, as well as the vineyard itself, piqued everyone's appetite. A visit to the tasting room provided the perfect aperitif to the scrumptious fare served on a patio overlooking the vineyard. Conversation about the many differences between East and West Coast cuisine soon leads to other observations. The degree to which California varies in something so fundamental as driving etiquette surprises everyone at the Ryders' table.

As lunch draws to a close, Brian stands up and requests everyone's attention. It is time for an overview of the wine country.

Vineyards in Napa Valley, northern California.

The Wine Country

"Sixty miles north of San Francisco, virtually at the same latitude as the Loire Valley and the city of Bordeaux in France, the most esteemed wine-making region in the world, we find California's own wineries vying for the same status.

"Viniculture began in Europe and was imported to this region in the late eighteenth century by the Spanish missionaries, who introduced grapevines to the new world to cultivate their sacrament. When the missions declined between 1820 and 1840, so did wine production, but the Gold Rush made this slowdown short-lived. Much later, Prohibition also put a temporary damper on large-scale wine-making, but the perfect climate, outstanding valley soil, and the continued immigration of sophisticated European viniculturists made growth inevitable. In the ensuing decades, many of the tools and techniques that had been passed down from the Middle Ages were scrapped to make way for technological advances.

"The advent of the large, mass-production wineries such as Paul Masson, Almaden, and Gallo has been facilitated by the efficiency of these modern techniques and equipment. Many of these wineries represent some of the oldest labels in the state. Despite the decline in quality usually associated with mass production, these companies have turned out what are usually considered excellent "jug" wines—wines made from mixing different grapes. Where the smaller wineries earn more awards in competitions, it is the large vintners who have had the greatest role in introducing the American public to the delights of California wine."

Once back on the bus, the seat rotation does indeed place the Ryders closer to the prime vantage point of the front windshield. For the first hour, however, a nap takes precedence over any sightseeing. The anticipation and early start of this day robbed many in the group of a precious hour of sleep, and this hour's grace period from touring and comment is much appreciated.

When they awake, the bright rays of the wine country have given way to muted sunlight flittering through the giant redwoods. The director speaks:

"Here in northern California redwood groves, it should be mentioned that for most of the century these trees provided the economic sustenance of the region. This was especially true during the postwar housing boom, which saw the perfection of the chain saw. In this vein, you may have the opportunity to view the Pacific Lumber Company located in the town of Scotia, just off 101 in Humboldt County. This factory town is worth a special look for a perspective on the oldest—1856—and largest redwood logging enterprise in the world.

"In recent years, cutting restrictions have put a damper on logging revenues, inspiring the adage that underscores the dilemma of the redwood economy: One person's conservation is very often another's unemployment. Nonetheless, as one passes through such areas as Richardson Grove State Park and Founder's Grove, it is difficult to conceive of harming these living fossils.

"A walk on the nature trails of the aforementioned preserves is highly recommended. Near Founder's Grove, look for the high water marks left over from the flood of the Eel River in 1964."

At this point, the bus stops and the Ryders spend forty-five minutes wandering through Founder's grove. After picture stops and a walking tour in this natural cathedral, the tour director continues his talk on the redwoods.

The Coastal Redwoods—*Sequoia Sempervirens*

"When Jesus was a boy, when Hannibal crossed the mountains with his elephants, the redwoods of today were already centuries old. During the Ice Age, redwoods covered two thirds of the North American continent and flourished in such unlikely locations as current-day Colorado and Texas. When the climate changed, many of these trees disappeared. Yet, enough remained to shape a great part of America's history. Pioneer babies rocked in redwood cradles, transcontinental trains traveled over red-

A giant redwood grove on Highway 101, California.

wood railroad ties, and redwood telephone poles carried American voices from sea to shining sea.

"As you walk through one of the many redwood groves along Highway 101, your voice will be muted in the presence of these redwood cathedrals. Footsteps will make no sound here, so thick is the ground cover. And looking up, the light may appear green and diffuse, as though peering through the murky depths of the ocean. Occasionally, a single shaft of light emerging through the trees gives the impression that the heavens are shining down.

"And why not? The select groves of redwoods in northern California are truly blessed. Growing only in a 500-mile long, 30-mile strip between Monterey County and the Oregon border, they draw upon a unique combination of the coastal fog and the strong California sun. Even though older and larger trees exist, none combines both qualities in quite the manner of the California redwood. Some of the sempervirens in the grove exceed two thousand years of age and top out well above three hundred feet. A single tree may yield over 490,000 board feet of lumber, enough to build twenty homes. To get a better idea of the size of redwoods, consider that many of these giants are twice as high as Niagara Falls and others eclipse the Statue of Liberty's torch.

"The botanist's name for redwood is Sequoia and was chosen to honor a blind Cherokee chief who invented an alphabet for this tribe. The coastal redwood is called, *Sequoia sempervirens*, the second half of the name meaning "forever living." Its counterpart in the Sierras, *Sequoia gigantea*, is usually older and wider but not as tall or widespread.

"As for the preservation of these Ice Age forests, the annexation of the redwoods to national parklands and private ownership through the auspices of the Save the Redwoods League has brought the logging of these giants to a low ebb. Although the bill for preservation has been costly to the lumber industry and American taxpayer, the alternative would have left the human race poorer beyond measure for generations to come."

Carson Mansion, Eureka, California.

As the sun's rays filter through the trees, our tired but still inquisitive group of travelers cruise through the factory town of Scotia, home of the world's largest redwood logging mill—the Pacific Lumber Company. Afterwards, they motor past the pastoral settings of the dairy country outside their home-for-the-evening—Eureka, California.

The director then concludes with some remarks on Eureka and its surroundings:

"Eureka, the capital of the redwood empire, is the only deep-water port between San Francisco and Seattle. Commercial fishing for salmon, Dungeness crab and petrale sole thrives here. Eureka is also the home of the most photographed house in the country, the Carson Mansion. This Victorian palace was built by William Carson, a local lumber baron in the late nineteenth century. It is the crown jewel of Old Town, a restoration of the glory that was Eureka during the heyday of redwood logging when she was a thriving port on the Humboldt Bay.

"Del Norte County, north of Eureka on Highway 101, is scenic enough to have served as a big-screen backdrop many times over. Here the redwoods meet the sea, while elk preserves, golden poppies, and Easter lily nurseries line the highway. Fishermen come to ply their trade in the Klamath River, famous for its salmon and steelhead.

"The last large town one encounters in northern California is Crescent City, whose half-moon bay was inundated by a tidal wave in 1964. Today, the town's offshore waters are kept calm by 1,600 tetrapods, huge five-sided interlocking concrete weights. As you pass through town, one of these sample wave-breaks is on display.

"Nearing the end of the Redwood Highway is a good time to reflect upon the demographics of the nation's most populated state. It is hard to believe that 26 million souls reside here, given the dearth of people in northern California. It is fortunate that the majority of California's populace lives to the south, for the land of giant trees and Chablis could not exist within the freeways and subdivisions of California's southland. The same can be said for the small-town charm of "California as it was" that you have just experienced along the Redwood Highway."

Prior to heading into the hotel, the group visits the city's turn-of-the-century Victorian restoration, Old Town. As they face the ornate gingerbread of the town's original centerpiece, the Carson Mansion, the Ryders reflect upon all they saw and experienced that day. This home of a redwood lumber baron would have been construed as the highlight of the day had they not toured the giant trees and Chablis earlier. Now all these aspects of their first day on the road fit into a mural whose parts harmonize.

It is at this point that our tour companions appreciate their agent for choosing this company and an itinerary that balances sightseeing, creature comforts, and the diverse concerns of several dozen mature travelers.

To celebrate their successful first day of the tour, Brian hands out a poem to each of the tour travelers.

A Poem of the Redwoods

Here, sown by the creator's hand,
In serried ranks the Redwoods stand,
No other clime is honored so;
No other lands their glory know.

The greatest of earth's living forms,
Tall conquerors that laugh at storms,
Their challenge still unanswered rings
Through fifty centuries of kings.

The nations that were with them young,
Rich empires, their forts far flung,
Lie buried now, their splendor gone;
But these proud monarchs linger on.

And so shall they live, when ends our day,
When all our crude citadels decay.
For brief are the years allotted man,
But infinite these perennials stand.

This is their temple, vaulted high,
And here we pause with reverend eye,
With silent tongue and awe-struck soul;
For here we sense life's proper goal.

To be like these, straight, true and fine,
To make our world, like theirs, a shrine.
Sink down, O Traveler, on your knees;
God stands before you in these trees.

—Joseph B. Strauss
Builder of the Golden Gate Bridge

Now You're Ready

With all these foregoing helpful hints for happy touring at your fingertips, you are now ready to take advantage of North

America's many exciting travel possibilities. The second half of *Bus Touring* will provide a window on the leading destinations that are available to you.

That we live in a land of contrasts requires little elaboration. North America is a continent of great geographical and cultural diversity. Nevertheless, travelers often base their expectations of a particular region upon their experiences of a vastly dissimilar area. For example, tourists viewing the spectacular wilds of Alaska become dismayed not to find the same luxurious amenities encountered on their Hawaii tour; or members of a New Orleans-bound charter might complain that the roadside scenery lacks the same breathtaking views of the Northwest landscape.

The lesson is clear. Each tour is a separate entity containing its own highlights and unique appeal. Properly prepared, you know what to expect and will not be disappointed. Unfortunately, some of this route-specific information is not often readily available from your travel agent or from most travel literature.

To bridge this gap, the following chapters detail eight popular touring corridors in North America. These regions are based upon the routing practices of the major tour companies. "The Golden Gate to the Glaciers" chapter, for instance, highlights the common practice of combining a northwest itinerary with western Canada. In similar fashion, the "Autumn in New England" section focuses on the northeast during peak touring season.

For each touring corridor, regional weather, comfort, shopping, cuisine, flora, and fauna are fully addressed. Reference is also made to sites common to many itineraries in each region. While some effort is made to elaborate upon these specific destinations, this section does not purport to be a guidebook. With travel agents and books as well as tour directors to fill you in on history, local color, and the like, the "Tour Planner" is more concerned with general trends.

These roadside observations are of a cross section of North America as viewed from a bus window. They are the result of interviews with guides who toured the areas in question for many years. Nonetheless, seek out a second opinion whenever possible. Above all, keep the following perspective on whatever pre-tour expectations you may develop: ultimately, an open mind and an accepting spirit is more important to a successful tour experience than the most informed preconceptions.

II

Cruising the Continent: A Motor Coach Tour Planner

CHAPTER 4

Points of Departure: Seattle, San Francisco, New York

"Location, location, and location." That recipe for business success also applies to the tour industry's choice of certain cities as tour gateways. While scenic beauty, history, culture, and creature comforts help determine where a tour begins and ends, the final choice depends on where the prospective gateway is situated on the map.

Some cities have all the luck. From Seattle tour travelers head north to Alaska, south to traverse the Oregon Trail, and east to the Canadian Rockies. From San Francisco they motor north to Chablis and giant trees, south to the beaches and deserts, and east to pan the Sierra for the last bit of gold. From New York they follow the path of history and fall foliage up and down the Eastern seaboard. Topping this, each of the tour industry's leading points of origin is privy to special coast-to-coast airfares. Add the excellent municipal mass-transit systems for access to urban adventures in dining and culture, and you can understand the "buscapade" that graces these tour gateways each year.

Seattle

Shaped like an hourglass, eighty percent surrounded by water, and built on seven hills, the sight of Seattle's Emerald Empire against the snowcapped backdrop of Mount Rainier sufficiently explains the popularity of this tour gateway. That is not to say that Seattle is just another pretty face. Whether for transport or tourism, Seattle's location is the essence of her success. At first this port of call was the point of embarkation for the Alaska/Klondike gold rush. Nowadays, it's more likely to be the golden opportunities for the tourist in search of the last frontier or a Rocky Mountain high.

Weather

The major worry in beginning or ending a tour in Seattle is that the deeper into September you get, the more you'll be playing dice with the weather. Contrary to what you might think, this is not so much a function of the rain as of the lack of sunshine. Although Seattle's forty-inch yearly rainfall doesn't rank above the totals in New York or Miami, a high percentage of days without sunlight, October to April, can put a damper on sightseeing and spirits. Nonetheless, the Emerald Empire is for the most part, a study in moderation. With neither the killer humidity of the Big Apple nor the cold fog of the Bay area, you can look forward to a majority of sunny days in the seventies from June to September.

Ambience

Seattle has always been a boomtown. The city started out as a logging center to fuel the housing boom occasioned by California's gold rush. Later, between Alaskan gold and oil and the trade opened up by the Panama Canal, Seattle's window-on-the-Pacific picked up where previous bonanzas had gone bust. Although many of the forces that jump-started Seattle's economy have come and gone, the friendliness and lack of pretension traditional to frontier hospitality are lingering effects of their legacies. There is also the ethnic diversity of a port city and a cultural consciousness reflected in the fact that Seattle has the most bookstores per capita of any major city in the country. And best of all for our purposes, Seattle is smaller in size, cheaper in price, and more casual in dress than most other tour gateways.

Sightseeing

The Seattle itineraries of major tour companies feature such attractions as the University of Washington campus and arboretum, the 600-feet-high Space Needle, the historic Pioneer Square neighborhood, and the Pike Place Public Market. The latter three attractions are located within a five-minute free bus ride of each other. This makes them conducive to independent exploration.

Although a transient population permeates the waterfront near the market and Pioneer Square, there is little to fear as far as personal safety is concerned. Moreover, there is perhaps no better microcosm of Seattle's history and personality than this area. Here, you can tour the original cityscape beneath Pioneer Square, visit the Park Service's Klondike Gold Rush Museum, and rub elbows at the market with the diverse peoples of the emerald empire.

Cuisine

When it comes to food in Seattle, the Pike Place Public Market tells the story. The cries of fishmongers, perfume of fresh-baked cinnamon rolls, and colors of fresh, moist produce greet the visitor on the main floor of this multitiered market. Unique seafood specialties ranging from Dungeness crab to squaw candy (strips of Indian smoked salmon) are pungent here alongside such coveted Northwest produce items as chanterelle mushrooms and

Space Needle Tower and Science Center, Seattle.

Yakima Bing cherries. Restaurants in Seattle draw from this horn of plenty and also feature award-winning wines of the region.

Shopping

For someone on tour, Seattle is a great place to shop. Pike Place and Pioneer Square offer everything from safari clothes to scrimshaw. If you're looking for a small, inexpensive souvenir evocative of the city, few items fit the bill better than Space Needle pens. The sight of a moving elevator superimposed on the pen's image of Seattle's distinctive tower is a compact reminder of this tour gateway. If bargains excite you, try the Pike Place Public Market for Alaskan smoked salmon. Because the processing of most Alaskan fish takes place in Seattle, prices here will often significantly undercut those further north. Best of all, the fish markets ship everywhere.

In addition to traditional gift items for friends and family, the existence of many outdoor clothing stores make this city a good place to outfit your trip. Popular regional apparel like Goretex rain-gear or Pendleton wool shirts are available from such nationally-known stores as Recreational Equipment Inc. (R.E.I.) and Eddie Bauer, which are headquartered in Seattle.

San Francisco

If you've been to San Francisco before, chances are you found the contours and the crowds of this city intriguing. Probably nowhere else in your travels did you see a town built on so many hills with so many diverse peoples in such a compact area. To be precise, the city is built on forty-two hills on a forty-five-square-mile peninsula. The 680,000 souls who inhabit this burgh live more closely together than the citizens of any other American metropolis. Another statistic that reflects the human face of San

Francisco is that this melting pot boasts thirty different foreign-language newspapers.

However, your most vivid impressions of the city probably will not be defined by a statistic. The lights of the city at night, the taste of the sourdough bread, and the smell of the sea air coming in with the fog are not conveyed in census figures or in an atlas.

Weather

Mark Twain is reputed to have said, "The coldest winter I ever spent was summer in San Francisco." Although its origin is still a point of contention, the truth of the assessment will not be lost on anyone who visits the city in July or August. At this time, evening temperatures hover around fifty degrees, and the wind and fog make it seem much colder. By contrast, daytime temperatures in late September and October average close to eighty degrees. At all times of year, you can expect morning fog and evening winds to eventually offset even the most severe heat wave.

It's important to remember that San Francisco possesses its own microclimate that is separate and distinct from the rest of the state. Therefore, prior to leaving the city, check reports in order to prepare for what is usually much warmer weather in the San Joaquin and Napa Valleys. This disparity can be so great that it's not uncommon to go from San Francisco's cold morning fog to hot sunny conditions minutes later after crossing the Golden Gate or Oakland Bay bridges.

Ambience

Much has been written about San Francisco and tourists. After all, tourists are the lifeblood of the local economy. As a result of tourism, the grit and noise of merchant marine activity and commercial fishing have been replaced by Fisherman's Wharf gift shops and restaurants. Other concessions to the needs of tourists are strict land-use and pollution control statutes. These

Bay Bridge in San Francisco.

have been partially responsible for pushing 85 percent of the heavy industry out of the city. In addition, millions of dollars are invested in such cosmetic make-overs as restoring the Victorian houses, historic buildings, and cable cars.

Despite the tourist trappings of this new development, the natural appeals of San Francisco remain undiminished. The hills overlooking the bay, the intimate restaurants that can inspire return-visits over a lifetime, and the *kulturfest* of ethnic neighborhoods and the arts will be here forever.

In San Francisco you can expect some of the highest prices anywhere and an Eastern formality in dress. New Yorkers will note other striking similarities between the two cities: parts of the skyline, the layout of the stores along Union Square, and the profusion of ethnic neighborhoods can evoke a *déjà vu*. Despite the big-city ambience, the effusive friendliness of the people here is a lot closer to the traditions of frontier hospitality. Whether the latter derives from San Francisco's gold rush heritage or from the city's vast experience with tourists, one thing is certain: it's easy to leave your heart in San Francisco.

Sightseeing

Although tour companies feature extensive San Francisco sightseeing excursions, these tours are not ends in themselves. Most programs here survey Fisherman's Wharf, Chinatown, Golden Gate Park, Sausalito, and other places that invite a visit on your own. More than any city on the continent, San Francisco is made for the independent traveler.

First of all, the inner city and greater Bay Area are accessible by a mass transit system unexcelled for variety and comfort. Options include bus, trolley, Bay Area Rapid Transit (BART, a clean, ultramodern subway), as well as two modes of transit that are attractions in themselves—cable cars and the Sausalito Ferry. The latter two offer significant discounts for seniors and some of the best views of the bay and the skyline.

Speaking of views, such rooftop lounges as the Top of the Mark and the Fairmount on California Street are the most popular for travelers on foot. City tour itineraries regularly feature the encompassing cityscapes offered by Twin Peaks and Fort Mason's bay-front panorama near the Golden Gate Bridge.

While mass transit and bird's-eye-views make it easy to get the big picture, the small size of the city and proximity of touristic haunts reduce San Francisco to a human scale. Since most of the points of interest you'll visit are on the cable car routes, I'll devote the major portion of the pedestrian perspective to these areas. Appropriately, a good place to begin is the cable car point-of-origin at Hallidie Plaza at the intersection of Powell and Market streets. Before you catch the cable car, stop in at the tourist information center at the station. Here you can find information on everything from city bus and trolley schedules to the opening and closing times of San Francisco's fascinating network of small museums. The fact that the plaza is home also to a BART station should be noted. Be careful about coming down to this area at night, however. On occasion transients from the neighboring Tenderloin district wander over into the plaza and create a ruckus. After the sun sets, you might prefer to catch the cable car in front of the Hotel St. Francis on Union Square.

Union Square is also a good place from which to set out for Chinatown, located several blocks away on Grant Street. On the way, window-shop Gump's, Neiman Marcus, and other temples of conspicuous consumption. In any case, your walking tour begins in earnest when you get to the top of Nob Hill, just up Powell Street from Union Square. From here it's a downhill walk to Fisherman's Wharf and the city's ethnic neighborhoods. You're also close to the rooftop watering holes at the Mark Hopkins and the "Fairmount" (a.k.a. the "St. Gregory"). If the view here leaves your legs too wobbly to trust yourself to walk the hills, there's always the California Street and Powell-Hyde/Mason cable car lines to carry you down to Chinatown or the bay-front. (The Powell Street line on the way back from the Mark lets you stop at Lombard Street. The "crookedest street in the world" offers special perspectives on Victorian homes, rhododendrons, and the Golden Gate Bridge spanning the bay.) By the time you get to the water, hopefully you'll have the sea legs to enjoy the Sausalito Ferry or the Blue and Gold Fleet's harbor cruise. Seeing the skyline from the water is especially dramatic and en route you'll also get close-ups of Alcatraz and the Golden Gate Bridge. The Wharf itself, while admittedly a haven of honky-tonk in recent years, is still good for stunning views, the best Irish coffee in the world (at the historic Buena Vista Cafe), and the harmonious discord of street musicians and performers. Apropos of the latter, it should be mentioned that comedian Robin Williams, as well as the mimes Shields and Yarnell, began performing to crowds at the Wharf in the manner of scores of other well-known dancers, musicians, jugglers, magicians, and singers. These performers and the curbside craftspeople must demonstrate special proficiency to obtain a license to ply their trades in the streets of San Francisco.

The preceding outline of an independent jaunt through the heart of San Francisco barely scratches the surface of all that is here to enjoy. To this end, I'd like to recommend one of the few guidebooks suited to the needs of the tour traveler—Jack Shelton's *Ten Perfect Days in San Francisco*, published by Chronicle Books. With a selective approach to "doing" San Francisco, the author is able to lace his potpourri of sightseeing tips with a very personal sense of place. Best of all, instead of just focusing on the inner city, *Ten Perfect Days* details the Bay Area and beyond. Itineraries include day trips to Muir Woods and the wine country and an overnite excursion to Yosemite. Wherever you're going, details on transportation, cuisine, and local color are given with a recommended pace for each day.

Cuisine

What can I say about the gastronomic delights of San Francisco that hasn't been said before? It's become a cliché among tour directors to tell their charges, "You can't have a bad meal in this city." With many more restaurants per capita and per square foot than any other American metropolis, such an assertion is impressive. As you will find, even the traditionally bland food served in big city hotel coffee shops can turn out to be gourmet fare. Most tours leave a high percentage of San Francisco meals to independent initiative. This is sometimes a function of cost, as well as the genuine desire to have the clients take advantage of diverse dining adventures. Usually, many recommendations are made by tour directors. These generally include a fish place on the Wharf, a five-star restaurant with a view, various ethnic eateries, and a place serving good old American food to give your tummy a rest.

Here are some miscellaneous tips that hopefully will serve you well. At seafood restaurants purveying fresh fish, be sure to have the waiter distinguish between "fresh" and "fresh frozen." In this vein, if you are inclined to experiment with such exotic denizens of the deep as abalone or Dungeness crab, make sure they are in-season. For quality "cheap eats," Chinese restaurants off of Grant Street are the best bet. And wherever you go, portions in this city tend to be larger than any other place I've seen, so pace yourself and wear loose-fitting clothes.

Shopping

Shopping in San Francisco can take on the aura of an olympic event. The endurance needed to climb the hills, together with the strength required to tote ivory chess sets and jade from Chinatown back to the hotel, could test the fortitude of the most intrepid decathlete. Even so, the greatest strain of all could be on your pocketbook. Hence, some advice.

Select indigenous specialties, because after taxes and inflation in America's most expensive city, it wouldn't pay to buy something here that you could find elsewhere. Give the curbside crafts a serious look. Due to stringent quality-control provisions in the city's licensing code, the artisanship is seldom in question. Best of all, the merchants' overhead for a storefront is not built into their price. The premier selection of outdoor marketplaces is on Hyde Street at Fisherman's Wharf and on Telegraph Avenue in Berkeley. Finally, don't hesitate to visit the Haight Ashbury section, whose dubious distinction dates back to the so-called hippie era. Instead of the seedy head shops of days past, tasteful gift items can be found in the interesting boutiques that now proliferate the neighborhood. In similar fashion, don't judge a book by its cover in Chinatown. Despite a superficially touristy veneer, the prices can't be beat.

One final shopping tip—always bring twice as much as you initially intended to spend if your itinerary will take in Union Square, the Embarcadero, and Sausalito. The trendy shops here give new meaning to the phrase "the sky's the limit!"

New York

Whether it's Radio City's communications vortex, the international marketplace of Wall Street, or the beacon of hope symbolized by the Statue of Liberty, New York has many distinctions befitting the sobriquet capital of the world. Not so well-known is the Big Apple's status as the East Coast's leading tour gateway. On crisp fall days in late September and early October, this aspect of New York's personality is in ample evidence in midtown Manhattan nearly every morning. Hundreds of buses with such diverse locales as Cape Cod, Williamsburg, and Niagara Falls emblazoned on the marquees above the driver's window, cruise the boulevards en route to fall foliage and cradles of American civilization.

Before these tours and after, there are the lights of Broadway, the treasures of the art world, and romps through Central Park, as well as a multitude of other sightseeing meccas to visit. In short, you can sleep when you get home!

Weather

The majority of New York-based tours run from April to the beginning of November. During these months the weather is seldom an obstacle, although the humidity in the summer can also make for a stinging dampness when the mercury drops. If you forget, you'll be reminded the next time you step out in fifty-degree Manhattan morning weather and end up feeling as though you've just jumped into a cold lake.

Ambience

New York has gotten an undeserved "bad rap" as a tourist's nightmare. Its size is undoubtedly foreboding and the pace at times unnerving, yet this is a city with a heart.

Take the subject of New Yorkers' reputed unfriendliness. Superficially, the sight of crowds jostling each other on the way to work supports this stereotype. However, if you are in need of directions, you probably could not find a more helpful and concerned urban population than this one.

There's also the impression that New York is all hustle-and-bustle without "people spaces." Such a notion can immediately be dispelled right in midtown Manhattan at St. Patrick's Cathedral. Pause and reflection are inherent to Central Park, as well as to the skating rink and mall at Rockefeller Center, both a few blocks away.

The danger of walking city streets here is often exaggerated also. Certain Manhattan neighborhoods (where tourists seldom go) after nightfall are veritable "battle zones," but you have little to fear if you use common sense. This means avoiding Central Park after dark and walking in groups of two or more in isolated streets.

Whatever your other expectations of New York, you will not be at all surprised to find many things here ethnic and eclectic, expensive and elegant, and in terms of scale, always exceptional.

Sightseeing

If you've never been to New York, chances are you won't be content to see the city from a bus window as you leave town in the morning. And given the problems attendant to Manhattan traffic and parking, that's just what you'll get in most packages with departures from here. While some companies subcontract Gray Line, most tour operators leave New York-sightseeing to independent initiative. And with the possible exception of Washington, D.C., there are few tour gateways on the East Coast as conducive to a self-guided excursion. It's a good thing, too. Instead of spending potential sightseeing time in bumper-to-bumper traffic, you can get to know the Big Apple intimately on foot. This means that a comfortable pair of walking shoes are *de rigueur*.

Unlike many Western cities oriented around the car, there's lots of sidewalk space here. The interesting people you'll pass and the opportunities to window-shop and people-watch along the way make the process of getting where you're going a treat in itself.

At the same time, be forewarned—crossing the street in this city can be a rude shock if it's your first time in the East. Unlike much of the rest of the country where pedestrians often have the right-of-way, in New York you'll live longer if you wait till the intersection is completely clear before crossing. The marvels of this city make up for this game of Russian roulette. However you go, be sure to plan an itinerary and a pace in line with your energy level. The less intrepid, for instance, might prefer the short walk in midtown (see what was said about people spaces in "Ambience") without fear of fatigue. The diehards can walk several miles from midtown Manhattan to such downtown and Lower East Side meccas as Greenwich Village, the Financial District, and Soho. These areas are particularly good places to get a sense of how the old and the new exist side-by-side in New York. On Spring and Greene Streets in Soho, for instance, you can take in cast-iron buildings from the mid-eighteen hundreds and then regain your twentieth-century bearings in the trendy boutiques and contemporary galleries nearby. The old and the new are again charmingly juxtaposed at the World Trade Center and the South Street Seaport Museum in the Financial District. After viewing the skyscraper contours of modern New York from the Trade Center, venture a few blocks over to the East River where restored ships and artifacts from the port city of centuries past are on display.

And what of the romantic cityscapes so often portrayed as a story setting or a big-screen backdrop? Whether it's the old-world elegance of traditional Manhattan interior decor or dramatic perspectives on the skyline, it's not hard to feel like you're an extra in a grand epic here. My own favorite places to play

The incomparable New York City skyline.

make-believe are New York hotel lobbies. The Plaza Hotel near Central Park might recall for you "Crocodile Dundee" or the home of Eloise. At the Algonquin Hotel, in the Broadway theater district, it's easy to imagine the New York *literati* of an earlier era convening to share coffee and creative ferment. As long as we're back in midtown, I'd be remiss not to mention the Empire State Building. The observatory is open every day, and the Thirty-fourth Street ticket office will let you know how much of the potential fifty miles of visibility there is to see on that particular day. While not as high as the World Trade Center, the consensus is that the view is more dramatic.

To complement the views from terra firma and above, take the Circle Line boat tour from Pier 83 on the Hudson River. It goes around Manhattan, providing perspectives on the United Nations Headquarters, the Statue of Liberty, the Cloisters Museum of Medieval Art, and the glittery spire of the Chrysler Building.

After seeing New York from the air, the land, and sea, and taking in the Manhattan mystique, you are now ready to pursue your special interests in depth. For culture vultures and music mavens, there are Lincoln Center, the Museums, and Broadway, to name but a few; for those in search of ethnic eateries, there are Chinatown and Little Italy; and for connoisseurs of the urban experience, there's a city that never sleeps.

Cuisine

Everyone knows that New York is a gourmet's paradise. What a lot of people don't know is that New York's humble fare boasts indigenous specialties. One bite of a bagel here and you'll taste what I'm talking about. Some say it's the water here that makes the difference. Speaking of which, it might surprise you to know that New York taps into the runoff of the Adirondack Mountains, giving it some of the purest drinking water found anywhere. Its similar status vaunted as a leading dairy state might also explain why such coveted national brands as Haagen-Dazs Ice Cream and Dannon Yogurt are produced here. New York State's famous MacIntosh apples and wonderful wines should also clue the traveler in that New York State comprises more than the canyons of Manhattan alone.

In any case, some of the best writing on food in this burgh are the books by Calvin Trillin (notably, *American Fried*, published by Random House), who also addresses this subject in his columns in *The New Yorker* magazine.

Shopping

While shopping in New York is a world wherein small specialty shops offer an array of quality items perhaps unmatched anywhere in the country, don't miss the large department stores—notably Macy's and Bloomingdales. Macy's, on Thirty-fourth Street, has the best prices. Nonetheless, it's worth a trip to the huge Bloomingdales store on Fifty-ninth Street, if only to admire the grand-scale displays and luxury items. In this vein, it should also be mentioned that the extravagance of "Bloomie's," Tiffany's and Cartiers is counterbalanced by good buys on apparel, books, and electronic items all over the city. If you're a "shopaholic," bring an extra suitcase.

Beginnings and Ends

First and last impressions are enduring, so get to know your itinerary's tour gateway. An exciting place to explore on your own, this city can stimulate reflection on an upcoming or just-completed journey.

Kamloops
Lake Louise
Banff
Calgary
Vancouver
CANADA
Victoria
Seattle
WASHINGTON
Bonneville Dam
Portland
Newport
OREGON
Coos Bay
IDAHO
Eureka
CALIFORNIA
NEVADA
San Francisco

CHAPTER 5

From Golden Gate to the Glaciers: San Francisco to the Canadian Rockies

In 1986, Americans discovered their own continent. Due to both aggressive promotion to "See America First" and instability abroad, Americans spent well over $200 billion on domestic travel. Perhaps no other region benefited more from this bonanza than the Pacific Northwest. With Expo '86 in Vancouver, British Columbia, attracting more than twenty million people, the ripple effects were felt from San Francisco to the Canadian Rockies.

While Expo '86 may have focused attention on the Pacific Northwest as a traveler's paradise, tourists have always come in great numbers to this region. The area boasts spectacular coastal and mountain scenery, cities that rank among the most romantic ports of call, and some of the best summer weather to be found. As such, many of the itineraries between San Francisco and the Canadian Rockies are venerated among the grand tours of the hemisphere. Indeed, with such routings as California's wine country, the Oregon coast, and Alberta's Icefields Parkway, merely stepping aboard a motor coach in this emerald empire guarantees a successful tour.

Weather

Figuring out the best time to travel in the Pacific Northwest is

Some of the best summer weather to be found is in the Canadian Rockies.

complicated by the unpredictability of the weather. What's more, morning fog near the ocean, desertlike conditions in Oregon, Washington, and British Columbia just east of the Cascade mountains, and the possibility of a summer snowstorm in the Canadian Rockies make packing a difficult chore. In fact, it's possible to experience the climate of each of the four seasons within the course of a trip from San Francisco to the Canadian Rockies.

Luckily, outside of encountering coastal and mountain storm fronts in the beginning and end of the tour season, the prevailing summer weather patterns are some of the best. Daytime temperatures range in the 70s and 80s, with less humidity than the rest of the country. Evenings are always cool. Unlike the East Coast and Midwest where a hot day continues into the night, here temperatures drop to the low 50s and sometimes reach freezing level in the higher mountains. Therefore, bring primarily light, casual clothes for the summer and fall months, including a wrap for that walk after dinner. Across the border, Victoria, Vancouver, and the Rockies necessitate a dressier evening wardrobe. In any case, the region as a whole puts a premium on flexibility. People

In Banff, elk can often be spotted peering inquisitively at a passing tour coach.

are quite active here, and formal dress requirements are inconsistent with their outdoor lifestyle.

Ambience

Despite the charm of the region, the long distances between sightseeing venues and creature comforts, crowded facilities in the Canadian Rockies, and changeability of the weather can create serious duress for the unprepared. To be specific, the 600 miles between the Rocky Mountains and the Pacific Ocean require considerable *sitz fleish* (sitting power) on the Banff to Vancouver itinerary. With a relative dearth of comfort stops and quality hotels along the way, most companies cover the mileage in two days. A few tour operators break up the long hours on the coach in western Canada by incorporating C.P. Rail's sleeping cars on parts of the route.

The need to cover ground in large increments is also very much present in the American Northwest and in northern California. This can be unsettling for folks from the Eastern seaboard who are used to passing through several states in a few hours.

It's become so crowded in the Rockies that many tours have no alternative to a buffet-style breakfast and lunch. With the anticipated rise in park visitation and the legal limits on concession development, do not expect this to change.

Roadside Attractions—Animal/Flower/Foliage Visibility

Although exceptions do occur, the best time to encounter animals near the highway is in the spring and fall when fewer people are on the road. During the spring, animals are just emerging from hibernation. In the fall, they are fattening up for the winter at elevations where you can see them from a motor coach. Your best bets in May to October for bird and wildlife viewing include:

Oregon: migratory waterfowl on the coastal estuaries; sea lions in the Sea Lion Caves just north of Florence; and salmon. In May and late September, most tours visit the Bonneville Dam fish ladders and viewing windows to observe the fish spawning.

Victoria: Beacon Hill Park offers views of sparrows, chickadees, gulls, cormorants, and other diverse land and sea birds.

The Rockies: mountain goats all through Banff townsite; bears near Jasper townsite or on the Icefields Parkway; moose off Icefields Parkway in wet areas; and bighorn sheep on high escarpments off the Icefields Parkway.

If you are a flower lover, the optimum time for your passion is the second week of June, providing you aren't bothered by the throng of kids beginning school vacation. At that time, California's golden poppies, Oregon's seaside rhododendrons, and Rocky Mountain lupine bloom along the popular tour routes. Portland's Rose Festival and the Butchart Gardens' peak season also take place during this period.

Despite the region's lack of deciduous trees, in comparison to the dense oak and maple forests of the east, the month of September offers scarlet hues of the vine maple and dogwood that break up the greenery of the evergreen forests. Vancouver's Stanley park is particularly spectacular at peak foliage time. Later in the month, the gold leaves of aspen that proliferate the higher regions of western Canada are a breathtaking sight. In October in California's wine country, the grapevines are ablush with color. This is the time of the first crush, and the aroma is as intoxicating as the multihued grape leaves. On the Northwest mountain ranges, wildflowers display their glorious colors all summer long. Indian paintbrush, bear grass, and vetch are particularly eye-catching here.

Besides an isolated California gray whale sighting in the very early spring and late fall of this season, schools of orcas (killer whales) are occasionally visible en route to Victoria from the mainland in late September.

Whatever the season, the chances of finding something for everyone might well be greater here than anywhere else on the continent. In western Canada, you will encounter a combination of English refinement in Vancouver and Victoria, pioneer heritage in rural British Columbia, and Alpine grandeur in the Banff/Jasper parklands. And on our own side of the border, you'll encounter cities renowned for their livability as well as such natural wonders as Mount St. Helens and the tallest and most extensive redwood groves in the world.

Cuisine

American Northwest and western Canadian itineraries offer culinary delights to suit diverse tastes. Alberta beef, Pacific salmon, Dungeness crab, and America's best outdoor produce market (Pike Street Market in Seattle) are likely to satisfy most gourmet palates.

At the same time, be forewarned of culture shock when it comes to certain foods. In the category of seafood for example, Pacific lobster and shrimp are considerably smaller than their East Coast counterparts. Carnivorous connoisseurs should be advised that the gamier texture of pasture-fed Alberta beef is less tender than U.S. Grade A from the feedlot.

Shopping

This region is one of the few parts of North America where you won't have to spend a fortune to get what most of us are looking for—something small that packs easily and is unique or indigenous. Redwood burl in Northern California; Myrtlewood clocks and bowls in Oregon; ready-to-ship vacuum-packed salmon in Washington; Shetland wool sweaters, bone china, and other English goods in Victoria; and Indian-carved jade trinkets and Cowichan sweaters throughout western Canada are among the quality souvenirs you'll have from which to choose.

Throughout the Northwest, you will also find good values on gold and jade, as well as semiprecious agates and geode-like thunder eggs.

General Advice

Here are some last pieces of advice. If you want letters and postcards to reach home before you do, don't send them by Canadian mail! Avoid sales tax by shopping in Alberta or Oregon—sales tax in California, Washington, and British Columbia run between five and ten percent. Don't expect to swim in the cold Pacific Ocean waters, even in northern California, and don't say "Frisco" and "Are-a-gone" instead of "San Francisco" and "Ore-gun" in front of Westerners if you're concerned about being identified as a tourist.

San Francisco
Yosemite National Park
NEVADA
UTAH
Monterey
Carmel
Big Sur
Hearst Castle
Morro Bay
CALIFORNIA
Las Vegas
Grand Canyon
Santa Barbara
Oak Creek Canyon
Sedona
Los Angeles
Montezuma Nat'l Monument
Scottsdale
Phoenix
San Diego
ARIZONA

CHAPTER 6

Valley of the Sun to Valley High: Scottsdale to Yosemite Valley

Superlatives. That's the only way to describe the land between Scottsdale, Arizona, and Yosemite Valley, California. This opinion is corroborated when we let the intelligentsia speak. Theodore Roosevelt called the Grand Canyon "the one sight that every American should see." John Muir referred to Yosemite Valley as "where America comes home."

American tour operators agree; their trade association's 1972 survey of statewide travel fantasies was dominated by California and her Southwest neighbors. According to the NTBA (now called NTA), the two natural wonders the American touring public most wanted to see were Arizona's Grand Canyon and California redwoods. In like measure, Arizona's Hoover Dam and California's Disneyland (pre-Orlando) were judged the most compelling man-made attractions.

Whatever significance one attaches to such rankings, it's not hard to figure out why this territory has always captured the fancy of the traveling public. The red rock and cactus of Arizona's canyon country, the glittery ambience of Las Vegas and southern California, and the rockbound coast of Big Sur can be enjoyed year-round. Indeed, there is perhaps no touring corridor in the continental United States that can combine such an easy-to-adjust-to climate with a veritable "who's who" of sightseeing meccas.

Weather

California—the very word literally means "earthly paradise." Along with a stunning landscape, California's Edenlike weather helped inspire her evocative name. The Golden State's relative absence of extreme cold and rain, plus the cooling effects of Pacific breezes, yields the country's mildest climate.

In a locale famed for sunshine, first-time visitors are often dismayed to find that coastal fog and urban smog occasionally threaten comfort and visibility. The haze really starts to be an obstacle to sightseeing when heat from California's inland valleys draws in a thick marine layer of clouds. This fog can last all day, obscuring such magnificent cliffside ocean vistas as Big Sur. Fortunately, those days when the coast is completely socked in are rare.

A difference in temperatures of thirty degrees or more between day and night can also surprise the newcomer. While this disparity is pronounced near the ocean and in the mountains, the desert often experiences the greatest fluctuations. Summertime mercury levels often crack the century mark in both the Mojave and Sonoran Deserts. California, Nevada, and Arizona natives might tell you that the lack of humidity makes this heat bearable, but most tourists tend to disagree. Relief generally comes when the sun goes down, as well as during the August/September rainy season in Arizona. In any case, this is an air-conditioned world where much time is spent poolside. Thus, the heat turns out to be less of a factor than one might initially suppose.

As might be expected, alpine areas such as Yosemite and the Grand Canyon experience the coldest weather on many

"Eye of the Sun"—on a Navajo reservation in Monument Valley, Arizona.

itineraries in this touring corridor. During the eight-month peak tour season (mid-March to December) morning frost is common in the early spring and late fall in both parks. Barring unforeseen cold snaps, these months constitute the only times you might need an overcoat anywhere from Valley of the Sun to Valley High.

Finally, I'd like to address a common misconception of first-time visitors to West Coast beach areas. To put it bluntly, forget about swimming north of Santa Barbara unless you're a polar bear. Even though the beaches farther south have warmer waters, the Pacific here is still considerably colder than most Atlantic or Gulf Coast swimming areas.

Ambience

To say that the dress is casual in this region is an understatement. Consider that the Arizona state legislature has mandated the bolo tie preferable garb to the traditional four-cornered necktie. And in Las Vegas showrooms regarded by many as the last bastion of tuxedoed formality, the predominant mode of attire is now neat and casual; a jacket isn't required but it's not out of place, either.

This "neat and casual" designation also applies to many of the fanciest establishments in California's southland. Perhaps traditional urban dress is not in keeping with an ambience Johnny Carson once described as "eighty suburbs in search of a city."

In any case the typical Western city is considerably more spread out than the urban areas in other parts of the country. As such, it lacks the vibrant downtown core traditional to Eastern cities. Hence, pedestrian traffic and mass transit are at a minimum. The latter could inconvenience those on tour after disembarking the coach. Going shopping or visiting friends in Phoenix or Los Angeles might well involve a costly cab or a rental car.

Roadside Attractions—Animal/Flower/Foliage Visibility

Where else but in California are the road shoulders on interstate highways adorned with golden poppies and magenta ice plants? The purple-flowered jacaranda trees on many southern California streets add to this festive color scheme. Thanks to bright sun and morning fog off the ocean, coastal areas can sport a botanical bonanza all year long. By contrast, you'll mostly see wildflowers in the mountains and cactus blossoms in the deserts from March to mid-June. The culprit is the complete absence of rain during the summer, replacing the flowers and greenery with a parched landscape. One notable exception is the Colorado plateau near the Grand Canyon. After the August rainy season, the red penstemon and other bright flowers sometimes bloom at the same time as the aspen leaves are turning golden.

Throughout the west, fall foliage is generally a lackluster event. However, Yosemite, with its aspens and transplanted Vermont maples, stands out. The beginning of the second week of October seems to be when the color change occurs.

Those interested in wildlife can count on seeing deer in the woodland meadows of this touring corridor at any time of the year. While there are no other guarantees, there's a good chance to witness the yearly return of the monarch butterflies to the Monterey Peninsula in late October. This area also sometimes offers other wildlife viewing opportunities. Either sea lions, harbor seals, or sea otters are a good bet for itineraries taking Ocean Drive and the Seventeen Mile Drive between Cannery Row and Pebble Beach. Brown pelicans, great blue heron, various kinds of gulls, and pelagic cormorants are also commonly seen here.

Early spring wildlife enthusiasts might enjoy such rarities as a pronghorn antelope sighting on the way to the Grand Canyon, or a California gray whale migration. These sightings diminish after April and pick up again after October. The chances for this opportunity to see the fastest land animals in the hemisphere increase after October. Farther south, forget about the swallows at San Juan Capistrano. Their habitat has been pretty much usurped by

Some of America's most dramatic and breathtaking scenery can be found along the California coast.

pigeons and doves. As for the San Diego Zoo and the desert bird and wildlife viewing, get there early. Eighty percent of the world's animals are nocturnal, including almost all desert animals, so by midday there is considerably less activity.

Cuisine

New Orleans is associated with red beans and rice and Boston with clam chowder. While one dish is often synonymous with a particular locale, in the case of Los Angeles, a whole menu would be in order. Sample entrees might include kosher burritos, crepe suzettes (locally referred to as French enchiladas), and tofu-burgers. Southern California has replaced New York as the new "melting pot," according to *Time* magazine, and its indigenous fare runs the gamut from health food to haute cuisine. Within this diversity are certain pervasive culinary trends that also apply to the region, Valley of the Sun to Valley High.

You can expect the liberal use of condiments like garlic and peppers, derivative of spicy Mexican food. Another noteworthy feature of the cooking here is the tendency to parboil the vegetables for maximum vitamin retention. Another outgrowth of the regional passion with fitness and health is the popularity of low-cholesterol, lighter fare.

Lastly, few places in the world yield a more extensive selection of fresh produce, fresh fish, and local meats. Whether it's artichokes and abalone in Monterey or southwest spring lamb, California's agricultural colossus and Arizona's home on the range yield a horn of plenty year-round.

Shopping

The most popular items on the shopping list of people traveling in this region are Disneyland souvenirs, dried fruit, and native American art. The major problem encountered by shoppers Valley of the Sun to Valley High seems to be the sides of their suitcases giving way under the weight of all their purchases.

The prime shopping stops on California itineraries include the boutiques and galleries of Carmel and the import and craft shops in the Danish town of Solvang. Tours that stop in San Diego often provide the option to go twenty miles south to Tijuana for good buys on leather goods, Kahlua, and French perfume. In addition, there are low prices on the jewelry and blankets sold by the Indians on the street, but don't forget to bargain.

In contrast, there is no dickering on the high prices of Indian jewelry and blankets in Arizona; the Navajo and Hopi craftsmanship is unexcelled in these categories. The budget-conscious shopper will find affordable sand paintings, however, depicting scenes from native culture with different-colored grains of sand on a small canvas. Not only is this traditional native American art form inexpensive, but it is lightweight and flat enough to be accommodated in even the most overstuffed suitcase.

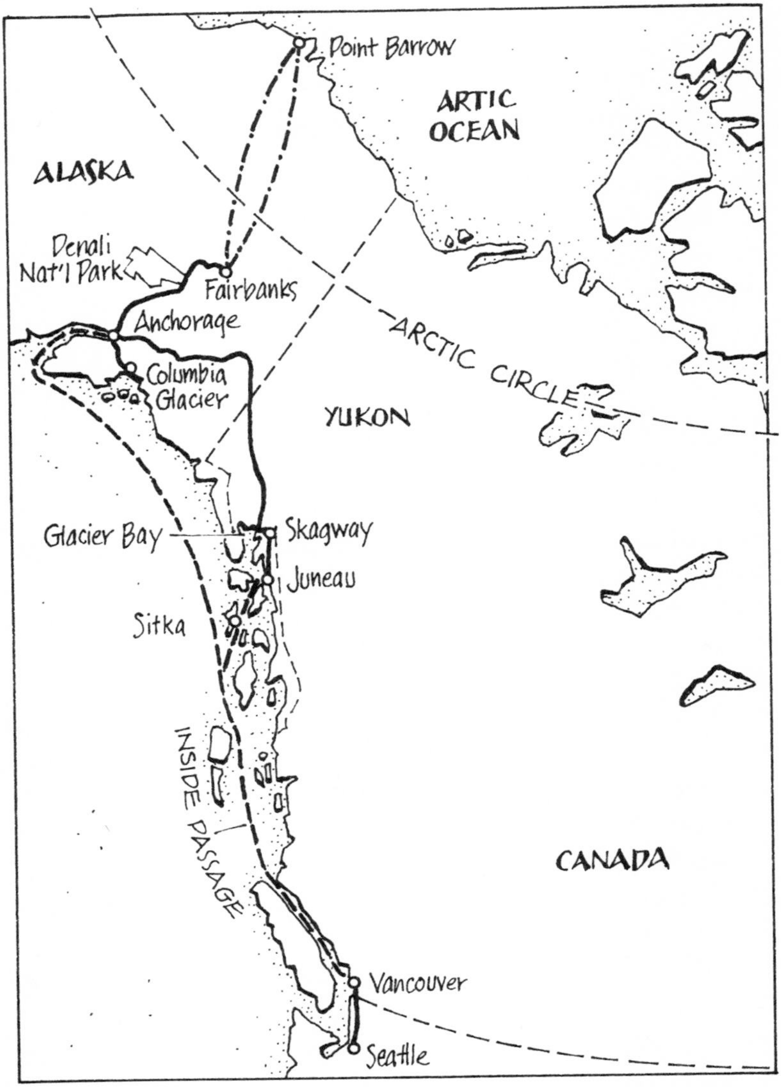
Point Barrow
ARTIC
OCEAN
ALASKA
Denali
Nat'l Park
Fairbanks
Anchorage
ARCTIC CIRCLE
Columbia
Glacier
YUKON
Skagway
Glacier Bay
Juneau
Sitka
INSIDE PASSAGE
CANADA
Vancouver
Seatlle

CHAPTER 7

A World Apart: Alaska

Whether you enter Alaska by air, land, or sea, one of the first things you'll notice is how much higher the mountains are than the big peaks of the Sierra, the Rockies, or the Cascades. This is the place to answer the call of the wild.

Mt. McKinley and environs is a good place to start. In the shadow of the continent's highest peak, more wildlife can sometimes be seen from a bus window in one day than would be in years of touring the rest of America's parks. Mountains' majesty and wildlife shows in this region are joined further south on the coast by glaciers that are unequaled for size and accessibility. For example, right outside the state capital, Juneau, you will find our country's only "drive-up" glacier, the Mendenhall, which sits in an ice field that is larger than the state of Rhode Island. The sky-blue color of these ice masses is best appreciated in Glacier Bay, however, where cruise ships regularly inch up on the world's largest aggregation of tidewater glaciers. Most Alaska travel packages supplement land transportation with an Inside Passage cruise, which also affords the chance to see whales, migratory waterfowl, and the highest coastal mountains in the world, the St. Elias-Fairweather range.

Touring in Alaska and the Canadian Rockies lets you enjoy a winter wonderland in summer.

With nature on such a grand scale, it's only fitting that there are people to match Alaska's mountains. The 800-mile-long, $8 billion Alyeska Pipeline is both evidence of a vital people, and a fount of touristic fascination. The art and culture of Alaska's native peoples and the remnants of Russian occupation bring more dimensions to the Great White North. The human touch is also felt in the preserved gold rush towns of Skagway and Dawson City.

Along with the works of God and man, in Alaska there is a chance to see the world in a unique and different light. Whether it's the multicolored rays of the aurora borealis in the fall or the shadows cast by the midnight sun in the spring and summer, a tour to the Great Land shines forth as the most exotic motor coach tour experience on the continent.

Weather

To most people who haven't been there, the word "Alaska" conjures only the Great White North. To those who know better,

America's forty-ninth state is many different worlds. These worlds range from the southeast coastal rain forests to the desert-dry Arctic. In between these realms, you can expect milder summer weather than in such tour meccas as Scottsdale, Arizona, and Williamsburg, Virginia where your clothes cling to you and the sun beats against your forehead like a sledgehammer. There is a preponderance of sixty-degree days during much of Alaska's tour season. And even though it gets cloudy quite a bit during the June to September peak visitation period, this actually has its own advantages. For one thing, overcast conditions are generally more comfortable for animals used to the predominant year-round conditions in the northerly latitudes—winter's endless night. In addition to being conducive to wildlife sighting, the muted light also brings out the blue tints on glacial ice, intensifying one of the visual highlights of any Alaska tour.

The exceptions to good traveling weather during Alaska's tour season include one week of ninety-degree temperatures in Fairbanks during June, July rainy spells in Anchorage, and cool wet weather everywhere between mid-August and late September. But even during these periods, conditions are seldom so severe as to inhibit sightseeing seriously in the Great Land.

A Special Note on Seasonal Phenomena

The best season for taking in the northern lights and unclouded views of Mt. McKinley is as late in the tour year (September) as possible. You can expect cold clear weather at this time.

Some folks with a penchant for numbers look to the four components of the so-called "Alaska sightseeing grand slam" as a measure of the success of their trip. If a tour is blessed by a grizzly bear, a whale sighting, a chance to see icebergs falling off tidewater glaciers into the sea (known as "calving"), and a clear view of Mt. McKinley, individuals count themselves as privileged to have tasted the quintessential Alaskan experience. Whether or not you care to quantify your visit in this manner, remember that only one out of seven people who tour here can claim an unclouded perspective on Mt. McKinley.

Ambience

The first time I went to Alaska I was surprised to find that Eskimos didn't rub noses or live in igloos, and Sergeant Preston of the Yukon never really existed. Over the years I observed the same naïveté in otherwise sophisticated travelers on their maiden voyage to the North country. But even when these folks' most romantic preconceptions are disappointed, they are still captivated by nature on a grand scale and the charm of Alaska's native peoples. This response is particularly impressive in light of the challenges posed by the typical Alaskan tour. To be specific, never have so many paid so much for so little in the way of creature comforts. Though this could be the most expensive tour you ever take on this continent, be prepared to rough it. Here's a look at what could happen in light of the worst expectations.

Rain, fog, long drives, and a lack of citified comfort are a function of the wildness and remoteness of the last frontier. On a two-week tour, you can realistically expect a little of each. The few roads that do exist are constantly being repaired, thus creating travel delays. The shortage of thoroughfares is best appreciated when you consider that the state capital, Juneau, cannot be reached overland by car.

Air-conditioning is not common in a place where for most of the year survival is a function of staying warm. As such, be prepared to sweat out an occasional ninety-degree day in Fairbanks if you're there in June.

Mosquitoes can make life miserable in the interior. Save your repellent for the smaller species, who are more voracious than their larger cousins.

As tour groups only have a limited choice of where to stay, overcrowding is endemic to certain hotels and restaurants. And, with two-thirds of Alaska's population living in and around

Panning for gold in Alaska.

Anchorage, rest stops in the Alaskan interior often require considerable ingenuity or perseverance.

The service and luxury one encounters aboard most cruise ships traversing the Inside Passage more than makes up for any inconvenience one might encounter during the land portion of an Alaskan tour. Although dress still remains decidedly casual, the majority of ships require dressing up for the captain's dinner.

Prior to the tour there is often considerable debate about whether you should do the cruise first before embarking on the land portion. Those who advocate heading north by boat point out that the saga of Russian occupation begins in the barrier islands of the Inside Passage, thus enabling you to follow Alaska's history chronologically. You also can get a feel for the progressive change of ecosystems as you head up from the mainland states. Those in favor of a southern cruise, point out that by flying into the interior and motoring south, you are reserving the last days of your tour, the time when you may be tired, for the slow pace and comfort of an ocean liner.

Whatever the logistics of your tour, Seattle is usually the tour gateway because connections are inconvenient to Anchorage or Fairbanks from the lower forty-eight. Appropriately, the fortunes of Seattle have been intimately tied to Alaska since the city began.

Another fact of tour life in the forty-ninth state is the preponderance of college students comprising the seasonal help in the hotels and restaurants. This work force has a refreshing friendliness. The human touch is also delightfully present in the Alaskan tradition of frontier vaudeville. Anchorage, Fairbanks, Skagway, Juneau, and Dawson City all feature Robert Service (bard of the Yukon) poetry readings, as well as musical and comedy productions relating to local color.

In short, you may not see the spit-and-polish efficiency here that characterizes many tours in the rest of the States, but a trip to Alaska usually offers so much variety and adventure that you willingly forego the comforts of home.

Roadside Attractions—
Animal/Flower/Foliage Visibility

Alaska's dramatic weather changes during the June to September peak travel season make the tracing of her plant and animal species a formidable task unless we confine ourselves only to certain species on the most commonly traversed tour routes. Even then, the complexity of the state's regional ecosystems often make very broad generalizations necessary.

Bring along some good binoculars. Remember that the best times for animal sightings are the twilight hours of sunrise and sunset. The state's most popular wildlife tour route through Denali Park departs before seven in the morning. During early June and late August is your best chance for seeing grizzly bear near Sable Pass. Denali Park is also where the willow ptarmigan (the state bird), caribou, Dall sheep, and moose are seen. The latter two species are also frequently sighted on the Seward Highway, which goes south from Anchorage to Portage Glacier.

Here and elsewhere, moose are most easily seen along riverbanks or among tall shrubs and saplings. Cows with calves abound in swamp areas in the first days of June. As for bald eagles, there's no place like Haines along the Lynne Canal to Skagway. In summer and fall they are also attracted to salmon spawning streams throughout the southeast and south-central part of the state. Several places off major touring routes to see the spawning phenomenon during mid-to-late August are: just before the Portage Glacier Visitor Center on the Seward Highway (known as Williwaw Creek), on Ship's Creek in Anchorage, and in the streams behind the Mendehall Glacier parking lot. Beaver lodges are easy to pick out halfway between Denali and Anchorage on the Parks Highway.

Whales can be spotted throughout the summer in offshore waters. Especially good places for this endeavor are Beluga Point for Beluga whales off the Seward Highway, the Lynne Canal in midsummer for pods of orcas and Dall porpoise, and the waters of the Inside Passage for all the above species, as well as humpback whales. Peak migration times are spring and fall.

Great flocks of birds migrate to Alaska in the early spring and can be seen easily in the southeast throughout the summer. An excellent place to spot such species as arctic terns, loons, and whistling swans is Potters Marsh on Seward Highway. In addition, the greatest array of migratory shorebirds in the hemisphere come to Prince William Sound at the end of the Inside Passage. These waters also feature whales, porpoises, and sea Puffin sightings in the heavily touristed areas are rare. Nonetheless, it's possible on occasion to glimpse these beautiful birds on the shoreline of Glacier Bay and the Lynne Canal in June, as well as on Prince William Sound throughout the summer. True aficionados will want to purchase *A Guide to Wildlife Viewing* in Alaska for $12.95. Send a check or money order to: Non-Game Wildlife Program, Alaska-Department of Fish and Game, Dept. AM 333, Raspberry Road, Anchorage, Alaska 99518.

Although Alaska's roadside bouquet does have its moments,

they are sometimes short-lived because of the severe conditions in the northerly latitudes. From the vantage point of a bus window, it's sometimes difficult to appreciate the many delicate flowers that grow low to the ground for warmth. Consider the state flower, the forget-me-not. These small blue flowers with an "eye" in the middle are virtually undetectable from the height of a touring vehicle. However, the folks who disembark the coach, at Denali Park's Polychrome Pass for instance, can often receive a wonderful perspective on these plants. This is not to imply that Alaska's roadsides are so devoid of color that one must always disembark the coach for close-up views. In addition to the chain-like yellow or blue lupine flowers, tour coach passengers will see the purple-blossomed fireweed on roadsides everywhere except in the Arctic, throughout much of the tour season. Peak time, however, for wildflower displays in Alaska is mid-June to mid-July.

Alaska's ornamental flowers and vegetable gardens are even more compelling for many people than her wildflowers. From July on, such gardens as the University of Alaska Agriculture Experimental Gardens at the Fairbanks campus can be a tour highlight if you're fortunate enough to "hit it right." Seventy-pound cabbages, roses that live for eighteen days after they're cut, and potatoes the size of footballs are not easily forgotten. Further south, Alaska's Matanuska Valley offers similar horticultural testimonies to the benefits of the midnight sun. Throughout the summer, marigolds with six-inch diameters and hydrangias that could pass for a cheerleader's pom-pom make up the floral displays on the streets of Anchorage.

Fall foliage is short-lived but spectacularly different. It generally comes and goes during the first week of September and is not restricted just to leaves on the trees. The real show occurs when the meadows take on red and yellow hues, due to lichens, grasses, and bushes turning. The golden leaves of the aspen and the scarlet dwarf birch add to this display.

Cuisine

Most food in Alaska is expensive and imported. Even most of the fresh fish from Alaskan waters is processed in Seattle. The latter is the saving grace of Alaskan cuisine. Traditional salmon bakes abound, featuring some of the most honest-to-goodness fresh seafood anywhere. Pundits on such matters maintain that king salmon from the Copper River, whose ferocious waters impart a heartiness to the fish, rates a royal salute for flavor. The cold Alaskan waters also yield such coveted crustaceans as Dungeness and king crab.

Garnishing your plate might also be potatoes, peas, cauliflower, or another vegetable from Alaska's Matanuska Valley. Produce from this region is distinctive for size as well as flavor. So much so that when locals joke about getting drunk on valley strawberries and feeding a family on one cabbage, you might be tempted to take them seriously. The rich soil and almost round-the-clock summer sunlight make the berries here quite juicy, and cabbages have been known to tip the scales at seventy pounds!

Reindeer sausage and other game meats are also common on Alaskan menus. Whatever you order, be prepared to pay top dollar. Keep the perspective that in 1987, a gallon of milk in Fairbanks cost $4.50 and was $7.50 above the Arctic Circle in Barrow.

Thus, if your itinerary only has a few meals included and dinner stops in remote areas, prices and such Eskimo delicacies as "muktuk" (whale blubber) can put a damper on the heartiest appetite. Nonetheless, the majority of Alaskan tour travelers can count on returning a few pounds heavier, thanks to cruise ship buffets and that ever-present dessert, baked Alaska.

Shopping

Alaska is the kind of place you can go for days without seeing a gift shop and then lo and behold, you find yourself awash in

Eskimo ivory carvings and Indian handwoven baskets. Prime shopping areas include: Fairbanks and Skagway for gold nugget jewelry, Eskimo carvings, and art prints; Sitka for smoked salmon and ivory; and Juneau for smoked salmon and T-shirts with Indian designs. These items can all be found in Anchorage along with jade, scrimshaw, and good prices on fur.

One more suggestion—if you're specifically shopping for authentic, native, hand-crafted items, look for the Silver Hand tag. Some investors say the latter will undoubtedly become collector's items on the order of Navajo and Hopi art in the southwestern United States.

CHAPTER 8

Southern Comforts: The Southeast

In 1986, the U.S. Travel Data Center reported that the southeastern part of the country recorded the largest number of visitors. The impression of a regional travel boom was compounded by the survey's selection of Florida's Disneyworld as America's leading tourist attraction. While the study also cited New Orleans' French Quarter and Opryland in Nashville as other big draws, the appeal of Dixie is not confined only to vaudeville, theme parks, and beaches. For nature lovers there's the fall foliage lighting up the Smokies as well as the floral displays of Alabama's Bellingrath Gardens. The history buff will find Civil War sites and antebellum homes lovingly preserved here. And those just "passin' through" will find a warm welcome from Southerners, who are famous for friendliness and hospitality.

Weather

If you are accustomed to a dry climate, you may want to avoid the region from mid-May through mid-September (most itineraries don't run this time of year anyway). Although air-conditioning is available nearly everywhere, you may still find the heat and humidity debilitating. Don't look for relief from the heat in a summer thundershower—it only makes the heat steamier.

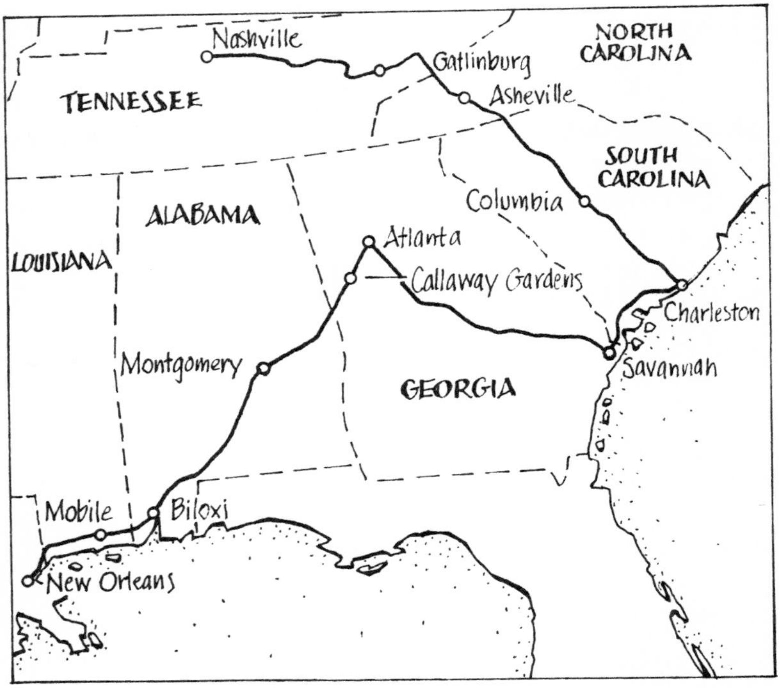

Nashville
Gatlinburg
NORTH CAROLINA
TENNESSEE
Asheville
SOUTH CAROLINA
Columbia
ALABAMA
Atlanta
LOUISIANA
Callaway Gardens
Charleston
Savannah
Montgomery
GEORGIA
Mobile
Biloxi
New Orleans

Some folks like heat and welcome the chance to bake the chill out of their bones on Mississippi's Biloxi beach. Most Gulf Coast beaches are swimmable from March to November. On the Gulf the temperatures stay hot or moderate through most of the year; you'll need a jacket only during the deep winter months. Inland, it gets chilly in mid-winter; bring a heavy coat. At the latitude of Memphis, even as far south as Jackson or Montgomery, there is a sizable snowfall with icy roads once or twice a year.

Visit in the spring if you can (but, unless you're interested in Mardi Gras, avoid being in New Orleans that week). The skies are clear and sunny, but the weather is still mild and provides the best chance to enjoy a series of real zippity-doo-dah days. The magnolias, dogwoods, and azaleas are in bloom, and the landscape, bare and brown in the winter months, takes on the appearance of a flowery paradise. This is the best time to view the variety of gardens that Dixie has to offer: Bellingrath in Mobile, Busch Gardens in Tampa, Magnolia Gardens near Charleston, or the Callaway Gardens in Pine Mountain (in Georgia).

Also within this period are pre-Lenten pilgrimages (mid-March to early April) on the Mississippi Delta. On these occasions, house and garden tours as well as parades help warm things up along with the changing weather. Finally, try to visit the natural attractions that the South offers during springtime, such as the Everglades of southernmost Florida or the Great Smokies that straddle the border between North Carolina and Tennessee.

Ambience

What images come to mind when you hear the word Dixie? If you think of cotton fields, strumming banjos, performers in blackface, and Scarlett O'Hara's plantation, then you share with many others the visual remnants of another era. The New South has little patience with faded stereotypes and, for the most part has relegated them to museums. If your mental images of the Deep South were formed by media events of the nineteen sixties or earlier, forget them. Today the South is probably further ad-

Oriental-American Garden, Bellingrath Gardens, Mobile, Alabama.

vanced in harmonious race relations than any other part of the country. It has long since ceased to be a plantation economy, and the region is now as culturally and economically diverse as any.

Dixieland lives on not only in memory but also in a few places that have taken pains to preserve their heritage. There are still traces of the Old South, if you know where to look or if you have a knowledgeable tour guide.

Southerners take three things especially seriously: sports, hospitality, and the Civil War. Spectator sports tend to be a bit more genteel here than in other parts of the country. At Old Miss and Auburn, for example, spectators dress up to attend a home football game. For other occasions, dress as you would anywhere else, appropriate to the weather. But if you really want to fit in with the locals, dress up for social occasions and on Sundays. A jacket-and-tie requirement for dinner is more common on Southern itineraries than in any other touring corridor in the country.

The fabled Southern hospitality is no joke; in general, people really are more gracious and friendly here than in other parts of the country. Take advantage of Southern gregariousness; you can learn a lot about a place by listening in on town-square gossip. On occasion it may be diplomatic and informative to while away a few minutes chatting with the check-out clerk or one of the good ol' boys at the service station. Don't be shy: Yankees and Westerners are welcome everywhere. But if you want to be utterly correct, refer to the Civil War as the War for Southern Independence. Some people are still sensitive about that. By the way, take note of the monuments to Confederate soldiers and to Confederate President Jefferson Davis that are found in public squares of many Southern towns.

There is no such thing as a Southern accent. Regional speech of the Southern states is distinctive, certainly. But there is a host of Southern dialects, each differing from another by as much as they differ from "standard" American English. You will hear many various accents, from Southerners who speak generic English, to those you may find nearly unintelligible. Anyway, to a Southerner, it's other people who have the accent.

Roadside Attractions

After dark in the summertime, watch the fireflies dancing or listen to the soft chirping of the katydids. During some parts of the summer, however, enjoyment of nighttime sounds will be sabotaged by the mating cries of cicadas. You can't imagine how loud an insect can be until you've heard a cicada calling in a nearby tree. Imagine a band saw in every tree and you'll get a fair idea.

During the spring and summer there is a wide variety of bird life to observe. Cardinals, bluebirds, woodpeckers—the South is blessed with extravagant bird colors. One of the first avian ambassadors you will hear is the drab-colored but tuneful mockingbird. There really is a bird that says tweety-tweety-tweedely-tweet!

On many inland roads of the South there is an extraordinary sight: the landscape is blanketed, trees and all, by an ivylike parasitic plant called kudzu. In some places it covers the countryside so thoroughly that the only way to know where a tree stands is by the shape of the kudzu mound. The plant was introduced as ground cover decades ago to retard erosion, and in many places it has taken over. In open fields where the kudzu has been beaten back, watch for cotton, sorghum, or tobacco, the most prevalent inland crops.

Much of the South is blessed with a commodity at a premium in other parts of the nation—clean air. On the other side of the balance sheet is highway litter. There seems to be a greater quantity of it here than elsewhere.

If you have an antipathy to shopping centers and four-lane highways, then look for itineraries that include backroads of the Deep South. Some of the finest, most unspoiled scenery is in the Southern Appalachian region of the Great Smokies and along the Natchez Trace, a well-maintained scenic highway through Tennessee and Mississippi. You can also escape from the twentieth century in the backwater bayous of Louisiana and on tours that incorporate "steamboating" on the Mississippi.

Surprisingly, the Great Smoky Mountains National Park, in Tennessee and North Carolina, is the most-visited national park in the nation (you thought it was Yellowstone, didn't you?). Most visitors, however, are headed for only one or two places of interest. If there are any places considered shrines of pilgrimage in the Deep South, they are four in number: Disneyworld in Orlando, Graceland (Elvis's mansion) in Memphis, Opryland in Nashville, and the Kennedy Space Center on Cape Canaveral. Most tourists in the Deep South take in at least one of these, but it is not necessary to visit any of them to catch the flavor of the region.

For a taste of the Old South, go to New Orleans, where the balconied courtyards of the Vieux Carre (French Quarter) have changed little since the eighteen forties, or Natchez, where antebellum mansions overlook the Mississippi River, or Savannah,

Oak Alley, built in the 1830s, between New Orleans and Baton Rouge, Louisiana.

a city of walled gardens and ironwork fence, or St. Augustine, the oldest city in the New World, or Charleston, for cobblestone streets and a waterfront promenade. The literary South also has appeal: New Orleans's French Quarter as Tennessee Williams saw it, and the Faulkner mansion in Oxford, Mississippi. For Civil War buffs, there are battlefields at Vicksburg, Shiloh, and Corinth, Mississippi. And if you're interested in historic homes, see the Hermitage outside Nashville (President Jackson's home), the St. John's Parish House in Savannah (occupied by General Sherman after his historic march through Georgia), or Jefferson Davis' home overlooking the Gulf in Biloxi.

Cuisine

Chitlins, hog jowls, pig's feet, hush puppies, black-eyed peas, okra and greens—most of these dishes can still be had at many Southern restaurants if you ask for them. On the whole, Southerners have abandoned these traditional delectables in favor of a cuisine that has more in common with the rest of the country. (The exception is grits, which is still a standard supplement to many Southern meals.) Inland, regional cooking is perhaps losing its distinctiveness as health-conscious Southerners demand less fried chicken and barbecued ribs and more salads and fish. Catfish has caught on in a big way and is abundantly supplied by Mississippi fish farms. Be sure to try fried catfish fillets; if you think of catfish as a junk fish, you're in for a pleasant surprise.

In New Orleans and many other places in the South, Cajun food, known for its spiciness and strong flavors, is popular. Don't insist on blackened redfish—a dish now in scarce supply because its extreme popularity a few years ago depleted the Gulf redfish population. Ask instead for blackened tuna, or some other common fish—it's even tastier.

Seafood is the culinary offering at which the South excels. The Gulf Coast has flourishing shrimp and crab fisheries, and its oysters are particularly tasty. Sample a plate of boiled crawfish if you can, although you don't need to "suck heads" as inveterate crawdad fanciers do. And be sure to try a selection of the finfish that the Gulf offers; grouper is a real treat.

Shopping

Shopping opportunities in the large cities—Atlanta, Mobile, Memphis, Little Rock—are no different from large cities in other parts of the country. Whether you find yourself on Peachtree Street in Atlanta or Biscayne Boulevard in Miami, you'll find many tempting souvenirs. A few places offer something truly distinctive—for instance the antique shops and the curiosity stores of the French Quarter and the artists that display their wares around Jackson Square in New Orleans. (Incidentally, if you look too obviously like a tourist in these places, you'll be a target for kids who seek to make a few bucks by betting you that they can tell you "where yo' got yo' shoes." Pretend you don't know the catch (yo' got 'em on Bourbon Street right here in N'awlins, that's where they standin') and bet a dollar; it makes for something to write home about.

In Charleston you may want to seek out handmade baskets in the open-air market. And Gatlinburg, Tennessee, is a mecca for Appalachian handicrafts. Otherwise, unless you're looking for antique furniture or Civil War mementos, you may find little that is regionally distinctive in most parts of the South.

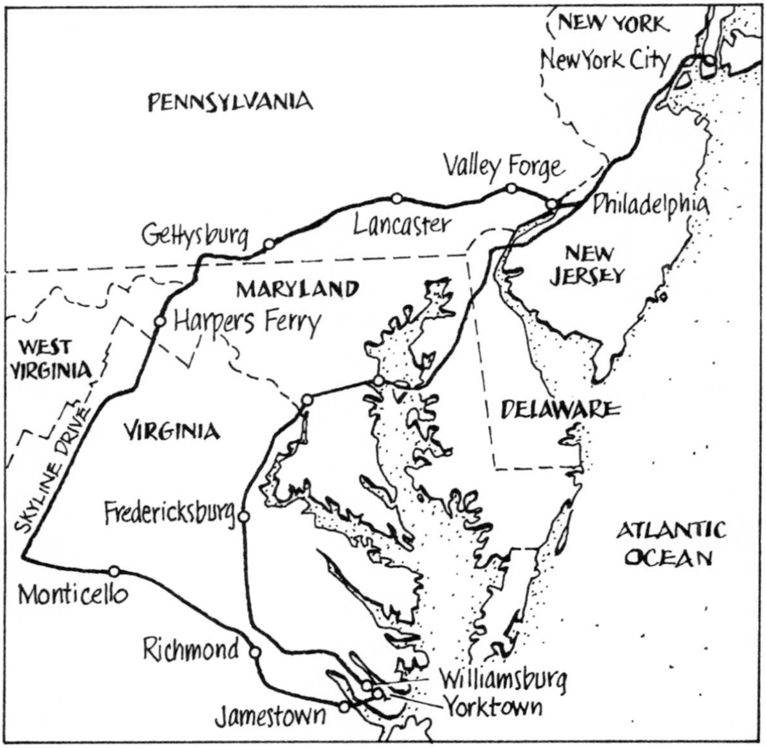

NEW YORK
New York City
PENNSYLVANIA
Valley Forge
Philadelphia
Gettysburg
Lancaster
NEW JERSEY
MARYLAND
Harpers Ferry
WEST VIRGINIA
DELAWARE
VIRGINIA
SKYLINE DRIVE
Fredericksburg
ATLANTIC OCEAN
Monticello
Richmond
Williamsburg
Yorktown
Jamestown

CHAPTER 9

Landmarks of Liberty: Washington, D.C., Virginia, and Pennsylvania

Visiting the historic sites and restorations in Washington, D.C., Virginia, and Pennsylvania is like meeting a relative you've heard about all your life, for the first time. The accounts you've heard since childhood often impart a *déjà vu* aspect to these encounters, and on occasion there is that spark of familial recognition that sends chills down your spine. And so it is with a tour of the shrines to colonial experience, the Revolution, the Civil War, and other landmarks of liberty. In such historic venues as Independence Hall and Monticello, the lofty words and deeds that we've read about resonate with greater force and meaning than ever before. Dramatic monuments and statues on the Washington Mall and at Gettysburg battlefield increase the impact of our heroic history. Finally, the Williamsburg Restoration and Philadelphia's Freedom Trail so engage the visitor with historically accurate re-creations, that the twentieth century seems far away.

Weather

This touring corridor is open from early April to the beginning of November, enjoying the longest season on the Eastern seaboard. Despite hot, humid conditions in the summer and occasional rain

America's most famous landmark, the Capitol Building in Washington, D.C.

during the otherwise idyllic spring and fall, extremes are seldom severe enough to inhibit appreciation of our heritage.

Ambience

Each year, thousands of group tours and student field trips follow America's story from the advent of the Jamestown colony to the signing of the Declaration of Independence. Although mature travelers and school groups may not always be compatible, it's inspiring to watch young folk soak up their American heritage. You might consider taking along a young member of your own family. No other tour in the United States points to as many parents and grandparents traveling with their offspring.

The nature of sightseeing in this touring corridor is markedly different from touring the West. The first thing you'll notice is that you can go through more than a half dozen states in the East in the time it would take to drive the length of California. While you're on the coach, the director is apt to be talking at an auctioneer's pace because there is so much history to cover.

Though the landscape is not on the grand scale that one finds west of the Rockies, it has a softer beauty due to the lower mountains and smaller deciduous trees. Something else common to many itineraries here is the free time left for independent sightseeing. The proximity of exhibits, buildings, and museums to each other in Washington, D.C., and Independence Mall, plus the shuttle bus system in Williamsburg, and plenty of Park Service guides at the historical sites can render your own tour director superfluous.

As for dress, there are pockets of formality within an otherwise predominantly casual ambience. In other words, pack a coat and tie if your itinerary features a group function in Washington, D.C., or Philadelphia.

Virginia

The drive between our nation's capital and Williamsburg, Virginia's colonial capital, is like a time machine voyage. From the

Colonial Williamsburg, Virginia, is like a voyage in a time machine.

wide boulevards and marble statues evocative of Paris in Washington, D.C., routes 395 and 117 carry you back to Old Virginia through forests, swamps, tobacco fields, and peanut plantations. Much of this route parallels the path of Washington and Rochambeau to Yorktown, which saw the British surrender and the end of the Revolution. An hour from the District of Columbia, the route traverses such Civil War landmarks as Manassas (Bull Run) where the Union and Confederate armies first clashed, and the battle-torn town of Fredericksburg, site of two major campaigns.

From this point on, you're apt to hear the Civil War referred to as the War of Northern Aggression, in accents which are a far cry from the chorus of foreign tongues common to the capital on the Potomac. You'll also see confederate and colonial flags prominently displayed from storefronts and front porches of homes whose claims to fame are ostentatiously etched in bronze. Inhabitants of the Old Dominion take their roots seriously, as is most evident in the Tidewater Peninsula, home to Jamestown, Yorktown, and Williamsburg. This spirit is also kept alive in Richmond, where statues and architecture pay homage to the capital of the Confederacy. Jefferson's home in Monticello and the South's Shenandoah Valley stronghold reinforce the impression of Virginia as the cradle of American civilization.

Pennsylvania

If Virginia lit the torch of liberty, then Pennsylvania certainly is the keeper of that flame. Ten square blocks of Philadelphia known as Independence Mall feature such attractions as the building where the Declaration of Independence was signed and the bell upon which the Fathers of our country let freedom ring in 1776.

Throughout the city, cobblestone streets and white-columned, red-bricked period architecture uphold the urban plan set forth by William Penn in the sixteen hundreds. Nearby Philadelphia, Valley Forge and Washington's crossing on the Delaware River are other chapters in the story of the battle for our independence. The Civil War era comes to life in the town of Gettysburg. Although the battlefield with its monuments, statues and museums is the chief attraction, the town itself features hundreds of landmark status buildings.

If your historical reverie is disturbed by the traffic and the noise of the Pennsylvania turnpike, the horse and buggy is still in fashion close by in the Amish country. Along with taboos on cars, electricity, and other modern conveniences, the Amish maintain an agrarian lifestyle in keeping with our colonial forefathers. Instead of television antennae and wires, hex signs and windmills adorn Early-American farmsteads here. When dusted with the first snows of late autumn, the Amish country landscape becomes the quintessential winter scene in the glass paperweight—the kind that becomes frosted with white powder when you turn it upside down. The major difference is that the pastoral setting in Lancaster County has remained unshaken by the outside world.

Roadside Attractions

The blossoms of spring and the fall foliage here, while not as varied or as widespread as New England's riot of color, still draw enough from Mother Nature's palette in each season to enhance touring profoundly. Indeed, in Washington, D.C., the Cherry Blossom Festival in early April, Skyline Drive's rhododendrons and azaleas at the beginning of May, and the mid-October changing of the leaves in the Blue Ridge rank among the most sublime outpourings of nature anywhere. In between these seasons, count on the Governor's Palace gardens in Williamsburg and the trees and horticultural displays around Monticello to enchant you.

Cuisine

The dining milieu that accompanies Williamsburg's colonial fare and the Amish country's home cooking can be as memorable as the taste of peanut soup and shoo-fly pie. In Williamsburg's colonial taverns, many tour groups dine amid period decor in establishments once frequented by the likes of Washington and Jefferson.

The ever-popular Pennsylvania Dutch Country's family-style restaurants have names like Plain and Fancy, where the traditional food is good and plenty and you leave fat and happy. This applies with equal force to a Maryland crab feed. Folks seem to enjoy this dish most with just a nutcracker and a bib around the neck to catch the drippings off this succulent shellfish. For the more sedate diner, Maryland crabcakes capture the flavor of the Chesapeake Bay.

Whatever the menu on your tour through Virginia, Pennsylvania, and environs, chances are you'll derive as much enjoyment from the setting as from the food itself.

Shopping

Gift ideas that bear the imprint of American heritage are quite popular among visitors to this touring corridor. Those in search of collector's items will find colonial-style pewter and furniture as well as antiques in the Williamsburg Craft House. The Amish handmade quilts also satisfy a penchant for traditional craft items.

In addition to having excellent books on the region's historic sites, Park Service bookshops carry a delight for civil and revolutionary war buffs—parchment copies of documents transcribed in the hand of the original signers. Traditional foodstuffs like Virginia ham and Amish relishes also have a following, but experience has shown the author that these are often acquired tastes.

Even if you don't make any purchases while shopping in this heartland of history, one thing is certain—the varied array of Americana on display will evoke the formative years of our country.

CHAPTER 10

Autumn in New England

Although an autumn in New England tour contains a rare combination of ingredients, the recipe is no secret. First, take the varied contours of a landscape broken up by mountains and rivers. Add a dash of rockbound coast, then sprinkle—liberally—with covered bridges and colonial architecture. After being steeped in the lore and history of early America, season with rusty-brown oak leaves, orange-red maple and pale yellow birch. Serve when there's a chill in the air. *Bon appétit!*

Weather and Roadside Attractions

Ecclesiastes's words "To everything there is a season" is good advice for anyone planning a New England tour. In fact, the region's fall-foliage itineraries rank as the country's most popular seasonal charter. Because it's difficult to predict when peak color will occur, here's some information that will prove useful whenever you go.

Let's begin by explaining why leaves change color. This phenomenon is the result of the muted sunlight that comes with the autumnal equinox. Thereafter, the production of chlorophyll —the chief nutrient chemical in the leaf—becomes inhibited, and

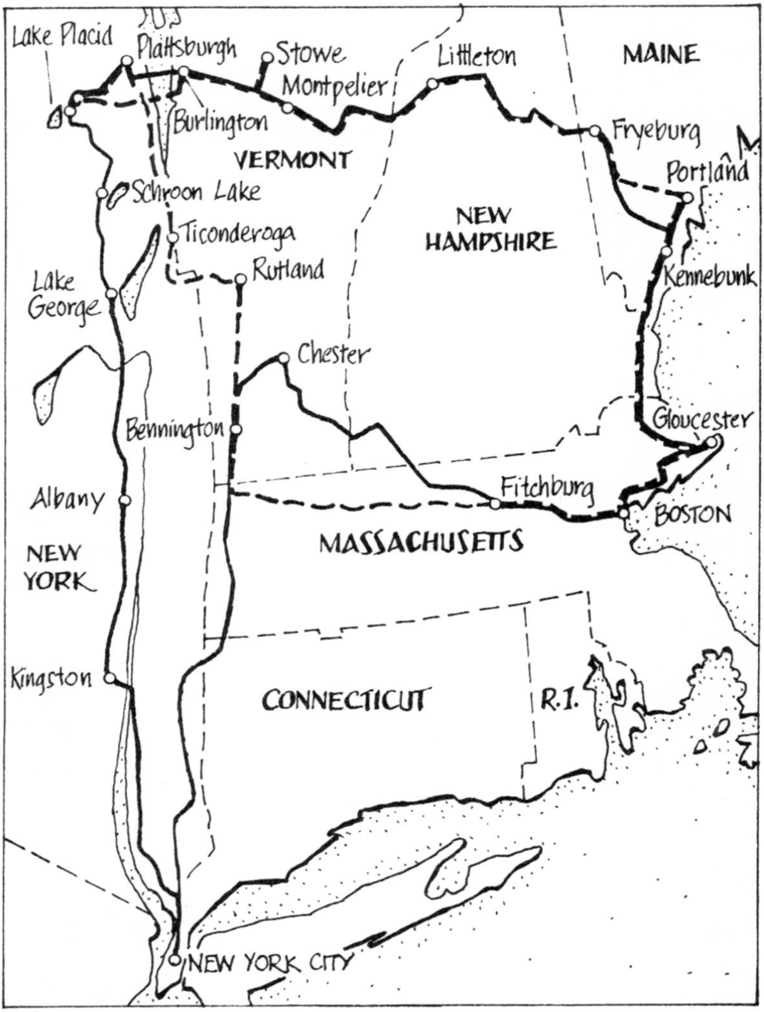

Lake Placid
Plattsburgh
Stowe
Montpelier
Littleton
MAINE
Burlington
Fryeburg
VERMONT
Portland
Schroon Lake
NEW
HAMPSHIRE
Ticonderoga
Rutland
Kennebunk
Lake
George
Chester
Gloucester
Bennington
Fitchburg
Albany
BOSTON
MASSACHUSETTS
NEW
YORK
Kingston
CONNECTICUT
R.I.
NEW YORK CITY

with it the dominant green pigment gives way to the red and orange colors of antocyanin and carotene. The end of this cycle comes when wind, rain, and cold conspire to bring dying leaves to the ground. Thus, lingering Indian-summer weather can delay autumn's glory, and a sudden severe cold snap can reduce the most spectacular foliage itinerary to a "twig tour."

Most foliage aficionados tour here between late September and mid-October to avoid these extremes. Even so, the display can vary greatly along the route. Late in October, for instance, bare trees in New Hampshire mountains might give way to luxuriant foliage in Connecticut, due to the warmer temperatures and lower elevations further south. Therefore, a varied itinerary spanning several states, climates, and topography assures you a portion of this visual feast at any time of the season. Due to its popularity, it's imperative to book this tour at least several months in advance.

Ambience

An autumn in New England tour experience is more than just the famed collage of color. While it's undeniable that the fall foliage provides an incomparable backdrop, the pageant of Americana that unfolds with each mile is never out of season. Consider this brochure excerpt describing a gambol through Vermont and New Hampshire.

"As Boston's steeples grow shorter behind the coach, you are crossing Massachusetts and rolling through its western highlands, the Berkshire Mountains. These are part of the Appalachian chain, as are the Green Mountains. In a while, we visit Newfane, Vermont.

"This small village may very well be the quintessential New England hamlet immortalized by generations of American artists. You have probably held it in your hand in the form of a Christmas card, and fondly in your mind as a place you always wished to visit—the peaceful village green, the snow-white steepled church, and of course, the general store where almost anything

Meeting house in Sturbridge Village, Massachusetts.

you ask for will be produced with a smile of confident pride. Toward day's end, reach Manchester, Vermont, there to dine and spend the night at a fully restored, classic country inn.

"This is a fascinating leg of your journey. It is perhaps best described as a Norman Rockwell day . . . visiting a venerable and authentic country store to taste homemade Vermont cheese, fudge batched up the way you remember it, striped stick candy, and many more tempting treats you don't approach at home. You'll take a gander into a farmer's museum, and amble along a whispering country lane to view the birthplace of President Cal Coolidge. Next, into Woodstock, the jewel of the Green Mountains—its village green shaded with elms and lined with unique craft and antique shops . . ." (Courtesy of Tauck Tours)

As you can see, the New England landscape is a Currier and Ives print come-to-life. It is only fitting to spend at least one night at an old New England inn. Replete with period furniture and a dining room featuring regional specialties, these cozy retreats let a tour group share a home away from home.

This feeling of communion is sustained by visits to some of the most written about shrines to our history. As you tour the sites of "The Shot Heard Round the World" and "Paul Revere's Midnight Ride," it's difficult not to feel as though you're on hallowed ground. In similar fashion, pilgrimages to historic homes let you walk in the footsteps of Louisa May Alcott, Nathaniel Hawthorne, Norman Rockwell, and other chroniclers of the American spirit.

Some of the most eloquent voices of the past are to be found, oddly enough, in the cemeteries of New England. Deathbed laments, black-humored doggerel, and poetic eulogies grace weathered headstones dating back hundreds of years. Another monument to New England's venerable legacy is its people. Possessed of the most distinctive regional mien of any part of the country, the image of the salty, taciturn Yankee has been firmly engrained in the American psyche for centuries. Nevertheless, autumn tour travelers are usually greeted here with polite friendliness. It's as if there's a generosity of spirit during harvest time to warm body and soul prior to the onset of winter.

In any case the Northeast is crowded compared to the rest of the country. To be precise, the Pacific Northwest takes up several times the area of the New England states but has but half the population.

Westerners will also notice pockets of white-gloved formality in the greater Boston area, as well as a jacket and the requirement in the dining rooms of some rural resorts. Daytime dress, however, puts a premium on comfort and functionality. After all, this is the home of L.L. Bean.

Most of all, the autumn tour traveler here should remember that these are unusually busy itineraries. In addition to several hundred years of history, art and literature, one need only look out the window at the technicolor roadsides to be thoroughly engaged. Expect early morning departures that take advantage of this horn of plenty, and get the jump on the "competition." Speaking of which, if you want to go at all, it's imperative to book this tour at least several months in advance.

Cuisine

Imagine yourself seated by a huge picture window overlooking the rocky Maine coast. A waiter comes forth to show the live lobsters he has in his pot for you and your tour companions. A short time later, you're enjoying a meal you'll recall in your minds-eye for years to come.

Later in the tour, there'll be other dining experiences. That bowl of milky-white chowder brimming with clams in a pewter mug will forever be inseparable from your image of the two-hundred-year-old inn not far from the Lexington Green. And the ski lodge vista of multihued treetops will be as fitting an accompaniment to your pancake breakfast as the hot Vermont maple syrup.

Even if you were to partake in less stimulating surroundings, Yankee cuisine by itself would still avail a bite-sized slice of New England life. The mere taste of maple sugar candy, Cape Cod salt-

Harbor on Cape Ann between Boston and Salem, Massachusetts.

water taffy, Vermont white cheddar, New England clam chowder, Indian pudding, scrod, Johnny cake, Boston cream pie, Parker House rolls, and Boston baked beans are as distinctly New England as the sound of dry leaves crunching on cobblestones underfoot.

Shopping

Let's face it—so much of what we buy in gift shops along tour routes ends up in the attic. Jugs of Vermont maple syrup, scrimshaw, Nantucket lightship baskets, and Norman Rockwell, Grandma Moses, and Winslow Homer reproductions are not so easily consigned to oblivion, however. These notions, along with the rest of the bounty from New England gift shops, could fill a veritable catalogue of cherished keepsakes and valued gifts. Shopping for craft items in Kennebunkport, Maine, sportswear in North Conway, New Hampshire, artwork in the mountains and on the shore of Massachusetts, as well as all manner of foodstuffs (cheese, syrup, apple butter) in Vermont are the best bets. Should you not find what you're looking for, chances are you'll encounter it in Boston or Cambridge, albeit at a higher price.

Even if you just end up window-shopping, a trip to Bostons' Quincy Market should quell any disappointment at going home empty-handed. The market's converted warehouses have spawned an array of interesting shops and eateries in the midst of Boston's colorful historic district. Such famed hotbeds of the revolution and colonial community as Faneuil Hall and the Old Customs House are a cobblestone's throw from the market stalls. In short, you have the prerequisites for time well spent.

Between Beantown's boutiques and other Yankee traders, you can count on shopping opportunities that far exceed the normal range of tour souvenirs. The best keepsake of all, however, is not found in any store. By taking a leaf ablaze with the glory of the season, dowsing it with hairspray, and pressing it between the pages of a book, you'll be able to preserve a remnant of this very special time forever.

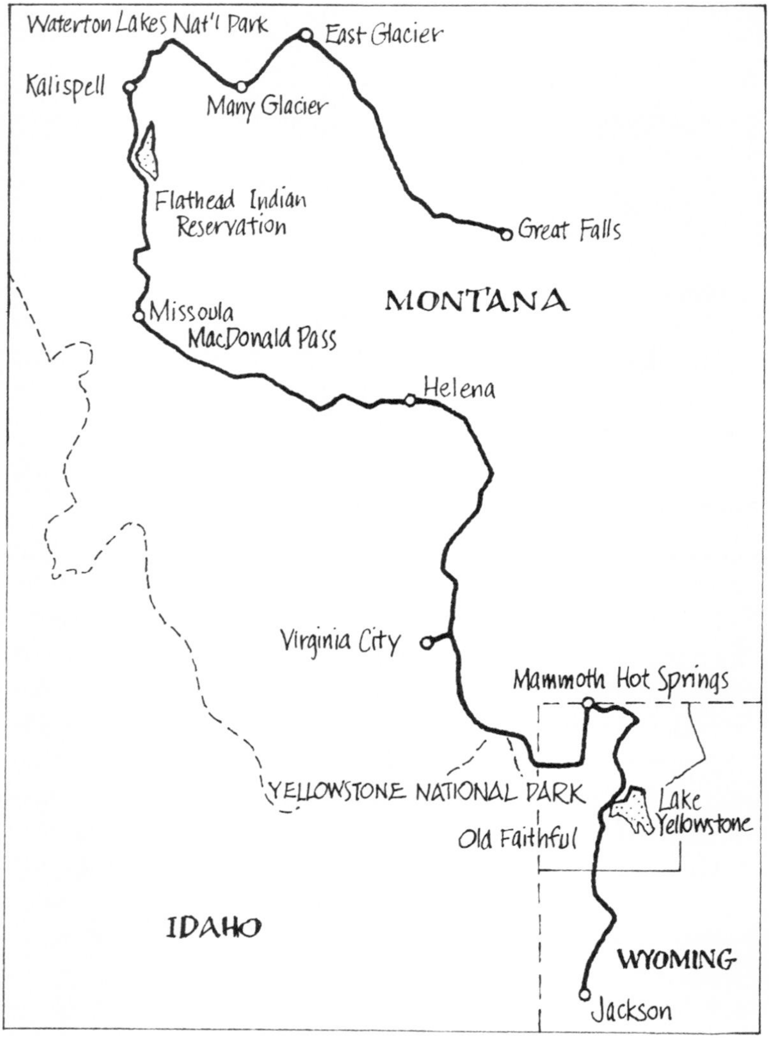

Waterton Lakes Nat'l Park
East Glacier
Kalispell
Many Glacier
Flathead Indian Reservation
Great Falls
MONTANA
Missoula
MacDonald Pass
Helena
Virginia City
Mammoth Hot Springs
YELLOWSTONE NATIONAL PARK
Lake Yellowstone
Old Faithful
IDAHO
WYOMING
Jackson

CHAPTER 11

Rocky Mountain High: Yellowstone, Grand Tetons, Glacier-Waterton Lakes National Parks

In 1872, Yellowstone was set aside as the first national park: "Preserved for the use of future generations." Perhaps no other gesture has had so great an impact on the course of American tourism as this governmental edict. The subsequent preservation of other parks bequeathed unto the touring public some of the most coveted shrines of pilgrimage on the continent. Among the crown jewels in this array are Yellowstone and its Rocky Mountain counterparts—Glacier-Waterton Lakes and the Grand Tetons. Despite their proximity to each other, these parklands have landscapes as different as the fire and ice that shaped them. The result is a touring corridor with the greatest variety of wildflowers, wildlife, and geological phenomena within the contiguous United States.

Weather

There's a saying in the Rockies: Only a dude or a fool predicts mountain weather. The north-central location and altitude of the Tetons, Yellowstone, Glacier, and environs subject tour travelers to a potentially greater range of weather than any other touring corridor within the lower forty-eight. It's possible to be influenced by air masses from Canada, westerlies on the storm track off the Pacific, or even fronts from the Gulf of Mexico. Those on tours that go to Glacier Park and points north might also experience a type of storm known as a chinook, characterized by abrupt record-breaking changes in temperatures and strong winds. In one strong chinook, temperatures rose thirty-seven degrees in four minutes.

Waterton Lakes, Glacier's Canadian counterpart, gets the bulk of the chinooks. Thunderstorms can happen anywhere and anytime in the northern Rockies, however, along with snowstorms in late August. It's a common practice among Yellowstone Park employees to celebrate Christmas on August 25 in recognition of this phenomenon.

When the weather is not in transition, expect warm days and pleasant nights in summer and crisp cold conditions in early June and mid-September. At all times you'll find mornings cool and locals reassuring you, "If you don't like the weather, wait ten minutes."

Ambience

Emerson said, "The wilderness can make a wonderful mistress but a difficult wife." The truth of this statement is perhaps best appreciated after a day of sightseeing here. Even though our spirits take flight while viewing Old Faithful geyser and the Teton's snowy spires, there is nothing so uplifting at day's end as the thought of a hot meal and a comfortable bed. In addition to the pleasure of creature comforts, many of us feel the need to return to the human perspective after seeing nature on such a grand scale. In any case, national park hotels are to the tour traveler what a light in the forest must have been to the pioneer family on a trek across the Wild West. Why, then, does recurring negative feedback about these establishments accompany many parkland itineraries? One reason is that few people realize that any development "spurious to the enjoyment of nature" is prohibited by law in American parks. With some exceptions, this has resulted in a very basic level of creature comforts at each preserve. Al-

Geyser Basin near Old Faithful, Yellowstone National Park, Wyoming.

though television, air-conditioning, and other amenities are rare, these places usually boast an exceptional natural setting. And even though the majority of the staff in park lodges is college students without professional experience, their shortcomings are usually compensated by friendliness and an eagerness to please.

Finally, the hotels themselves possess a warmth and distinctiveness that is often missing in more modern structures. Built of native stone and local wood to blend in with the surroundings, such famed hostelries as the Old Faithful Inn and the Prince of Wales Hotel have served the traveling public since the first decades of this century.

Yellowstone

Be that as it may, you are likely to be more interested with what's outside your hotel window than with what's inside. In Yellowstone you'll find a landscape of geysers and hot pools, a huge lake and a 300-foot waterfall backdropped by the yellow-rock canyon that inspired the park's name. Yellowstone is 95 percent back country, so the three million visitors who come June to September crowd the highways and concessions. The majority have come to see Old Faithful geyser, as well as the other manifestations of geology in action. Instead of the subtle inexorable expansion and contraction of the earth's crust, some of the land in Yellowstone literally bubbles beneath your feet.

Much of the park is situated on a plateau whose elevation exceeds the highest peak on the entire Eastern seaboard (Old Faithful is 7,700 feet above sea level), so be careful not to overexert. Pacing yourself in a park more than twice the size of Rhode Island (3,462 square miles), however, is not always easy—particularly because the array of geological phenomena, animal habitats, and plant communities is unequaled in any other park in the United States. Life is sustained here by ecosystems that run the gamut from dry sagebrush grasslands to alpine meadows covered with wildflowers. In between there are thick evergreen forests and rocky cliffs.

The Grand Tetons

The Grand Tetons may lack the diverse appeals of their illustrious neighbor to the north, but still manages to steal the show when it comes time to break out the album of tour pictures. Although photographing these mountains is the focal point of a tour group's experience here, there are enough things to do in the area to make the Tetons a mainstay of most northern Rockies itineraries. A visit to an elk preserve, a river float trip, or browsing the shops and galleries in Jackson Hole are all enjoyed in the shadows cast by these aptly-named mountains.

Glacier Park is more remote and less peopled than its sister parks to the south. Only one highway crosses the American portion of the park, Going-To-The-Sun Road. It has been called the most beautiful fifty-mile stretch of road in the world. The two-lane highway travels from the prairie and ascends into the mountains. After crossing the Continental Divide at Logan Pass (6,600 feet above sea level) the road then drops abruptly in a tortuous spiral en route to Lake McDonald. Spectacular wildflowers, waterfalls, grizzly bears, and mountain goats appear along the way to complement stunning views of the northern Rockies. This road is precipitous, so those with motion sickness should consider taking medication to combat it. The road is generally plowed and passable from mid-June to mid-October and is best appreciated early in the season or after September when there is less traffic and more animals.

The park's other delights range from boat tours on Swift Current Lake (which affords good views of glaciers) to some special opportunities for wildlife sightings. Glacier boundaries encompass the prime habitats for grizzly bears and bald eagles in the contiguous United States, as will be detailed in the next section.

Waterton Lakes

Since the nineteen twenties, bus tours have been running between Glacier and Waterton Lakes across the Canadian border. The two parks also share a common ecosystem, as well as hotels that were originally built by the Great Northern Railroad to encourage tourism in the area. These similarities together with U.S.-Canadian friendship prompted the establishment of Waterton-Glacier International Peace Park in 1932.

Despite these ties, Waterton avails the tour traveler a very different experience than comparable enclaves below the border. Without a network of roads going deep into the vast wilderness contained by the park, most itineraries confine themselves to the town of Waterton Lakes. Unlike American parks, Canadian preserves permit the existence of municipalities within their boundaries. Thus, tour groups stop off at this lakeside-resort town nestled in the mountains to take advantage of the last vestiges of citified comfort. On a windy bluff above the town and the lakes is the rustic Prince of Wales Hotel, where some groups have lunch and/or stay overnight.

But Waterton Lakes is more than just a comfort stop. First,

imagine twin alpine lakes from which the snowcapped Rockies rise up steeply. Within this natural amphitheater is a wildlife show that is truly exceptional for such a small area. Birds traversing the migratory thoroughfares known as the Central and Pacific flyways, elk herds, mountain goats, and bears are all commonly seen here.

Roadside Attractions

The group travel season in this touring corridor is very short, usually extending from mid-June to early September. This is due to road and concession closures as well as weather. Within this period, there are innumerable cycles of plant life and animal feeding/mating patterns that determine what you'll see from a motor coach. At all times, you can count on enough roadside attractions in the northern Rockies to necessitate keeping your camera constantly on the ready. Here's a rundown of the highlights on the major touring routes here.

In Yellowstone, look for elk and moose grazing on the algae around the geyser basins. September, the elk's mating season, is prime time for sightings. During the summer, many of the herds are visible in the forest meadows en route to the park's northern Mammoth region. Moose are best sighted in wet and swampy areas, such as the shorelines of Lake Yellowstone and along the banks of the Firehole River. Bighorn sheep can be viewed on the steep escarpments near Mammoth and on the cliffs paralleling the park's eastern entrance. Look for the grizzly bears in the Hayden Valley. Bison can be seen in this region, as well as in the northeast plains of the park. This dry region also attracts golden eagles in search of carrion. Black bears as well as Steller's jays can be found throughout the whole park.

As for flowers, the best roadside display is located on Dunraven Pass, which goes over Mount Washburn. The aspen forests on the north side of this mountain pass generally begin to change color in late August and reach their peak the first week of

September. The best display of all, however, comes a little later, when the Tetons become flecked with the gold leaves of this lovely tree.

Glacier Park's Going-to-the-Sun-Road is the major focus of attention for aficionados of Mother Nature's seasonal delights. In July, Logan Pass's alpine meadow repertoire of glacier lilies, Indian paintbrush, red monkey flowers, and mountain heath is breathtaking. The most eye-catching blossom of all, however, might be the white, bulbous beargrass. It occasionally attracts that otherwise shy denizen of the forest, the grizzly bear, down the roadside. Above Logan Pass Visitor Center, hoary marmots, which are related to prairie dogs, are commonly seen grazing on the lichens and sedges of the snowy, glaciated areas. On the other side of Logan Pass, mountain goats and bighorn sheep are often visible near an area known as the Garden Wall. In the lowlands of the park, all kinds of wildlife are seen ranging from bears in the meadows near Many Glacier Hotel to bald eagles, who come to the Lake McDonald area with the approach of fall.

Tourists prepare to embark for a scenic ride on Glacier National Park's Going-to-the Sun Road.

The latter migration is timed to coincide with the autumn run of Kokanee trout. Osprey are common around all lake areas.

In Waterton, look for bison near the park entrance and elk herds along the lakeshore below the Prince of Wales Hotel. Also note the mountain goats near Cameron Falls on the way into town. In September, migratory waterfowl on the Pacific and Central flyways stop for a breather here. As for the park's floral display, Waterton comprises one of the richest alpine botanical areas among the Canadian Rockies parks. The reason is due to its location on the crossroads between grasslands and mountain, enabling it to draw species from both.

Neither Banff nor Jasper have grassland species complementing alpine flora to such an extent. As such, Waterton's botanical display surpasses that of these better-known Canadian parks. Among the more common flowers, look for lupine in the meadows near Waterton's park entrance and bear grass blanketing the slopes near town.

For those who want to further appreciate Mother Nature's glory here, *The Field Guide to Rocky Mountain Wildflowers*, by J. and F. Craighead and R. Davis (published by Houghton Mifflin) is a definitive work. This tome supplies the only listing that maps the interrelationships between the season of bloom with wildlife phenomena. Instead of the usual guidebook designation, which might read "late June to early September," *Field Guide* has listings on the order of "Swamp-laurel blooms both when and where mosquitoes are becoming a nuisance." The efficacy of this method of organization is explained by Roger Tory Petersen in the "Introduction": "The Rocky Mountain region is a vertical land when spring and summer ascend the slopes, and a flower that blooms in June in the river valleys might not unfold its petals until July or even later at higher altitudes."

The book's color plates round out an outstanding treatment of the northern Rockies' ecosystems.

Shopping

Western-wear and "cowboy" art in Jackson Hole, precious and semi-precious stones in gift shops throughout the region, and Waterton's selection of Canadian jade, fur, and Indian cowichan sweaters are on many shopping lists here. Prices are high due to the tourist economy and the remoteness of the region. In Waterton Lakes, however, a favorable exchange rate and lack of sales tax make shopping a pleasure.

Cuisine

Buffalo burgers, Flathead Lake region cherries and Rocky Mountain trout are considered indigenous specialties. In the parks themselves, food quality is surprisingly good, considering the seasonal staff and the remoteness from distribution centers. Nonetheless, buffet breakfasts have become the rule, particularly in the crowded Glacier Park hotels.

Over the border in Waterton, the most significant departure from good old-fashioned American food is such English fare as Yorkshire pudding and trifle. This is derivative of the English settlement of western Canada.

Epilogue

The English travel writers of the past century traditionally closed their books with a through-the-porthole look at a distinctive landmark fading into the sun's last rays. These images were usually accompanied by an invitation to seek out the joys of the open road. But you don't have to be a vagabond on a tramp steamer to sample travel's golden moments.

Just ask any tour group who has seen the pink rays of sunrise against a glacier's snowy throne reflected into Lake Louise. Other groups might tell stories about standing on the Yorktown hill where Washington secured the British surrender.

And even if it's too foggy and rainy to fully appreciate these shrines, many tour groups create their own sunshine. The warmth and camaraderie on board a coach can actually transform an otherwise dreary day into an unforgettable experience.

I'll never forget one particular ride through a flood-ridden Mojave Desert between Las Vegas and the Grand Canyon. After a tour of the Hoover Dam was washed out by a cloudburst, we were delayed a half-hour due to a mud slide covering the highway. With clouds descending but voices raised in song, we climbed steadily out of the desert towards the 7,000-feet-above-sea-level elevation of the Grand Canyon rim. It was late in the tour season and in the day, and we hurried to get there by dark.

The mists that filled the canyon were as thick as anticipated. The swirling, gray tendrils of evaporating moisture seemed to extend down forever—except for a solitary clearing that exposed the Colorado River. Just when we got out to have a better look, a solitary shaft of sunlight revealed the multicolored rock strata of the place the Indians named Land of Frozen Rainbows. A minute passed, and just as suddenly as the rock had appeared, a new wave of clouds rolled in to cover it up again. My companions were overjoyed at the heavens' unexpected benediction. It seemed to me then, and now, as though Mother Nature herself was reaffirming that the success of a tour is not the destination, but the journey itself.

For Further Information

If you would like to get further information on tour operators or options available for bus touring, contact your travel agent or one of the following:

National Tour Association (NTA)
P.O. Box 3071
Lexington, KY 40596
(606) 253-1036 or 1-800-NTA-8886

American Bus Association (ABA)
1025 Connecticut Ave., NW
Washington, D.C. 20036
1-800-422-1400

American Society of Travel Agents (ASTA)
1101 King St.
Alexandria, VA 22314
(703) 739-2782

United States Tour Operators Association (USTOA)
211 E. 51st St., Suite 4B
New York, NY 10022
(212) 944-5727

Other Books from John Muir Publications

Asia Through the Back Door, 3rd ed., Rick Steves and John Gottberg (65-48-3) 336 pp. $15.95

Being a Father: Family, Work, and Self, Mothering Magazine (65-69-6) 176 pp. $12.95

Buddhist America: Centers, Retreats, Practices, Don Morreale (28-94-X) 400 pp. $12.95

Bus Touring: Charter Vacations, U.S.A., Stuart Warren with Douglas Bloch (28-95-8) 168 pp. $9.95

Catholic America: Self-Renewal Centers and Retreats, Patricia Christian-Meyer (65-20-3) 325 pp. $13.95

Complete Guide to Bed & Breakfasts, Inns & Guesthouses, 1990-91 ed., Pamela Lanier (65-43-2) 504 pp. $15.95

Costa Rica: A Natural Destination, Ree Strange Sheck (65-51-3) 280 pp. $15.95

Elderhostels: The Students' Choice, Mildred Hyman (65-28-9) 224 pp. $12.95

Europe 101: History & Art for the Traveler, Rick Steves and Gene Openshaw (28-78-8) 372 pp. $12.95

Europe Through the Back Door, 9th ed., Rick Steves (65-42-4) 432 pp. $16.95

Floating Vacations: River, Lake, and Ocean Adventures, Michael White (65-32-7) 256 pp. $17.95

Gypsying After 40: A Guide to Adventure and Self-Discovery, Bob Harris (28-71-0) 264 pp. $12.95

The Heart of Jerusalem, Arlynn Nellhaus (28-79-6) 312 pp. $12.95

Indian America: A Traveler's Companion, Eagle/Walking Turtle (65-29-7) 424 pp. $16.95

Mona Winks: Self-Guided Tours of Europe's Top Museums, Rick Steves and Gene Openshaw (28-85-0) 450 pp. $14.95

The On and Off the Road Cookbook, Carl Franz (28-27-3) 272 pp. $8.50

The People's Guide to Mexico, Carl Franz (28-99-0) 608 pp. $15.95

The People's Guide to RV Camping in Mexico, Carl Franz with Steve Rogers (28-91-5) 256 pp. $13.95

Preconception: A Woman's Guide to Preparing for Pregnancy and Parenthood, Brenda Aikey-Keller (65-44-0) 236 pp. $14.95

Ranch Vacations: The Complete Guide to Guest and Resort, Fly-Fishing, and Cross-Country Skiing Ranches, Eugene Kilgore (65-30-0) 392 pp. $18.95

Schooling at Home: Parents, Kids, and Learning, Mothering Magazine (65-52-1) $14.95

The Shopper's Guide to Mexico, Steve Rogers and Tina Rosa (28-90-7) 224 pp. $9.95

Ski Tech's Guide to Equipment, Skiwear, and Accessories, edited by Bill Tanler (65-45-9) 144 pp. $11.95

Ski Tech's Guide to Maintenance and Repair, edited by Bill Tanler (65-46-7) 144 pp. $11.95

A Traveler's Guide to Asian Culture, Kevin Chambers (65-14-9) 224 pp. $13.95

Traveler's Guide to Healing Centers and Retreats in North America, Martine Rudee and Jonathan Blease (65-15-7) 240 pp. $11.95

Undiscovered Islands of the Caribbean, Burl Willes (28-80-X) 216 pp. $12.95

Undiscovered Islands of the Mediterranean, Linda Lancione Moyer and Burl Willes (65-53-X) 224 pp. $14.95

22 Days Series
These pocket-size itineraries are a refreshing departure from ordinary guidebooks. Each author has an in-depth knowledge of the region covered and offers 22 tested daily itineraries through their favorite destinations. Included are not only "must see" attractions but also little-known villages and hidden "jewels" as well as valuable general information.

22 Days Around the World by R. Rapoport and B. Willes (65-31-9)
22 Days in Alaska by Pamela Lanier (28-68-0)
22 Days in the American Southwest by R. Harris (28-88-5)
22 Days in Asia by R. Rapoport and B. Willes (65-17-3)
22 Days in Australia, 3rd ed., by John Gottberg (65-40-8)
22 Days in California by Roger Rapoport (28-93-1)
22 Days in China by Gaylon Duke and Zenia Victor (28-72-9)
22 Days in Europe, 5th ed., by Rick Steves (65-63-7)
22 Days in Florida by Richard Harris (65-27-0)
22 Days in France by Rick Steves (65-07-6)
22 Days in Germany, Austria & Switzerland, 3rd ed., by Rick Steves (65-39-4)
22 Days in Great Britain, 3rd ed., by Rick Steves (65-38-6)
22 Days in Hawaii, 2nd ed., by Arnold Schuchter (65-50-5)
22 Days in India by Anurag Mathur (28-87-7)
22 Days in Japan by David Old (28-73-7)
22 Days in Mexico, 2nd ed., by S. Rogers and T. Rosa (65-41-6)
22 Days in New England by Anne Wright (28-96-6)
22 Days in New Zealand by Arnold Schuchter (28-86-9)
22 Days in Norway, Denmark & Sweden by R. Steves (28-83-4)
22 Days in the Pacific Northwest by R. Harris (28-97-4)
22 Days in Spain & Portugal, 3rd ed., by Rick Steves (65-06-8)
22 Days in the West Indies by C. & S. Morreale (28-74-5)

All 22 Days titles are 128 to 152 pages and $7.95 each, except *22 Days Around the World* and *22 Days in Europe*, which are 192 pages and $9.95.

"Kidding Around"
Travel Guides for Children
Written for kids eight years of age and older. Generously illustrated in two colors with imaginative

characters and images. An adventure to read and a treasure to keep.

Kidding Around Atlanta, Anne Pedersen (65-35-1) 64 pp. $9.95
Kidding Around Boston, Helen Byers (65-36-X) 64 pp. $9.95
Kidding Around the Hawaiian Islands, Sarah Lovett (65-37-8) 64 pp. $9.95
Kidding Around London, Sarah Lovett (65-24-6) 64 pp. $9.95
Kidding Around Los Angeles, Judy Cash (65-34-3) 64 pp. $9.95
Kidding Around New York City, Sarah Lovett (65-33-5) 64 pp. $9.95
Kidding Around San Francisco, Rosemary Zibart (65-23-8) 64 pp. $9.95
Kidding Around Washington, D.C., Anne Pedersen (65-25-4) 64 pp. $9.95

Automotive Books

The Greaseless Guide to Car Care Confidence: Take the Terror Out of Talking to Your Mechanic, Mary Jackson (65-19-X) 224 pp. $14.95
How to Keep Your VW Alive (65-12-2) 424 pp. $19.95
How to Keep Your Subaru Alive (65-11-4) 480 pp. $19.95
How to Keep Your Toyota Pickup Alive (28-89-3) 392 pp. $19.95
How to Keep Your Datsun/ Nissan Alive (28-65-6) 544 pp. $19.95
Off-Road Emergency Repair & Survival, James Ristow (65-26-2) 160 pp. $9.95
Road & Track's Used Car Classics, edited by Peter Bohr (28-69-9) 272 pp. $12.95

Ordering Information
If you cannot find our books in your local bookstore, you can order directly from us. Your books will be sent to you via UPS (for U.S. destinations), and you will receive them approximately 10 days from the time that we receive your order. Include $2.75 for the first item ordered and $.50 for each additional item to cover shipping and handling costs. UPS will not deliver to a P.O. Box; please give us a street address. For airmail within the U.S., enclose $4.00 per book for shipping and handling. All foreign orders will be shipped surface rate; please enclose $3.00 for the first item and $1.00 for each additional item. Please inquire about foreign airmail rates.

Method of Payment
Your order may be paid by check, money order, or credit card. We cannot be responsible for cash sent through the mail. All payments must be made in U.S. dollars drawn on a U.S. bank. Canadian postal money orders in U.S. dollars are also acceptable. For VISA, MasterCard, or American Express orders, include your card number, expiration date, and your signature, or call (800)888-7504. Books ordered on American Express cards can be shipped only to the billing address of the cardholder. Sorry, no C.O.D.'s. Residents of sunny New Mexico, add 5.625% tax to the total.

Address all orders and inquiries to:
John Muir Publications
P.O. Box 613
Santa Fe, NM 87504
(800) 888-7504
(505) 988-1680 FAX

Europe 101, Rick Steves & Gene Openshaw $12.95 (78-8) 372 pp.

The first and only jaunty history and art book for travelers makes castles, palaces and museums come alive. Both Steves and Openshaw hold degrees in European history, but their real education has come from escorting first-time visitors throughout Europe.

Asia Through The Back Door, Rick Steves & John Gottberg $11.95 (76-1) 336 pp.

In this detailed guide book are information and advice you won't find elsewhere—including how to overcome culture shock, bargain in marketplaces, observe Buddhist temple etiquette and, possibly most important of all, how to eat noodles with chopsticks!

Traveler's Guide to Asian Culture, Kevin Chambers $12.95 (14-9) 356 pp. Spring '89

Veteran traveler in Asia, Kevin Chambers has written an accurate and enjoyable guide to the history and culture of this diverse continent.

Bus Touring: A Guide to Charter Vacations, USA, Stuart Warren & Douglas Bloch $9.95 (95-8) 192 pp.

For many people, bus touring is the ideal, relaxed and comfortable way to see America. The author has had years of experience as a bus tour conductor and writes in-depth about every aspect of bus touring to help passengers get the most pleasure for their money.

Road & Track's Used Car Classics, edited by Peter Bohr $12.95 (69-9) 272 pp.

Road & Track contributing editor Peter Bohr has compiled this collection of the magazine's "Used Car Classic" articles, updating them to include current market information. Over 70 makes and models of American, British, Italian, West German, Swedish and Japanese enthusiast cars built between 1953 and 1979 are featured.

Automotive Repair Manuals

Each JMP automotive manual gives clear step-by-step instructions, together with illustrations that show exactly how each system in the vehicle comes apart and goes back together. They tell everything a novice or experienced mechanic needs to know to perform periodic maintenance, tune-ups, troubleshooting and repair of the brake, fuel and emission control, electrical, cooling, clutch, transmission, driveline, steering and suspension systems, and even rebuild the engine.

How To Keep Your Car Alive: A Basic Sanity Saver $14.95 (19-X) 208 pp. April '89

If you don't know a spark plug from a soup spoon, this book is for you. Gives the basic of how a car works, where things are and what they're called. Demystifies your auto and allows you to drive or talk to your mechanic with confidence. Color illustrations to enhance descriptions.

How To Keep Your VW Alive $17.95 (12-2) 384 pp. (revised)
How To Keep Your VW Rabbit Alive $17.95 (47-8) 440 pp.
How To Keep Your Honda Car Alive $17.95 (55-9) 272 pp.
How To Keep Your Subaru Alive $17.95 (49-4) 464 pp.
How To Keep Your Toyota Pick-Up Alive $17.95 (89-3) 400 pp.
How To Keep Your Datsun/Nissan Alive $22.95 (65-6) 544 pp.
How To Keep Your Honda ATC Alive $14.95 (45-1) 236 pp.
How To Keep Your Golf/Jetta Alive $17.95 (21-1) 200 pp. April '89

ITEM NO.	TITLE	EACH	QUAN.	TOTAL
-				
-				
-				
-				
-				
-				
-				
-				
-				
-				
-				

Subtotals ______

Postage & handling (see ordering information)* ______

New Mexicans please add 5.625% tax ______

Total Amount Due ______

METHOD OF PAYMENT (circle one) MC VISA AMEX CHECK MONEY ORDER

Credit Card Number ______ Expiration Date ___-___

Signature X ______

Required for Credit Card Purchases

Telephone: Office ( ) ______ Home ( ) ______

Name ______

Address ______

City ______ State ______ Zip ______

See reverse side for Ordering Information

ORDERING INFORMATION

Fill in the order blank. Be sure to add up all of the subtotals at the bottom of the order form, and give us the address whither your order will be whisked.

Postage & Handling

Your books will be sent to you via UPS (for U.S. destinations), and you will receive them in approximately 10 days from the time that we receive your order.

Include $2.75 for the first item ordered and add $.50 for each additional item to cover shipping and handling costs. UPS shipments to post office boxes take longer to arrive; if possible, please give us a street address.

For airmail within the U.S., enclose $4.00 per book for shipping and handling.

ALL FOREIGN ORDERS will be shipped surface rate. Please enclose $3.00 for the first item and $1.00 for each additional item. Please inquire for airmail rates.

Method of Payment

Your order may be paid by check, money order or credit card. We cannot be responsible for cash sent through the mail.

All payments must be in U.S. dollars drawn on a U.S. bank. Canadian postal money orders in U.S. dollars also accepted.

For VISA, Mastercard or American Express orders, use the order form or call (505) 982-4078. Books ordered on American Express cards can be shipped only to the billing address of the cardholder.

Sorry, no C.O.D.'s.

Residents of sunny New Mexico add 5.625% to the total.

Backorders

We will backorder all forthcoming and out-of-stock titles unless otherwise requested.

Address all orders and inquiries to:

JOHN MUIR PUBLICATIONS
P.O. Box 613
Santa Fe, NM 87504
(505) 982-4078

All prices subject to change without notice.